→INTRODUCING

BARTHES

PHILIP THODY & PIERO

Published in the UK in 2011
by Icon Books Ltd.,
Omnibus Business Centre,
39-41 North Road, London N7 9DP
email: info@iconbooks.co.uk
www.introducingbooks.com

Sold in the UK, Europe, South Africa
and Asia by Faber and Faber Ltd.,
Bloomsbury House,
74-77 Great Russell Street,
London WC1B 3DA
or their agents

Distributed in the UK, Europe, South
Africa and Asia by TBS Ltd.,
TBS Distribution Centre,
Colchester Road, Frating Green,
Colchester CO7 7DW

This edition published in Australia
in 2011 by Allen & Unwin Pty. Ltd.,
PO Box 8500, 83 Alexander Street,
Crows Nest, NSW 2065

Previously published in the UK and
Australia in 1999 and 2006

This edition published in the USA
in 2011 by Totem Books
Inquiries to: Icon Books Ltd.,
Omnibus Business Centre,
39-41 North Road,
London N7 9DP, UK

Distributed to the trade in the USA
by Consortium Book Sales & Distribut
The Keg House
34 Thirteenth Avenue NE, Suite 101
Minneapolis, Minnesota 55413-1007

Distributed in Canada by
Penguin Books Canada,
90 Eglinton Avenue East, Suite 700,
Toronto, Ontario M4P 2Y3

ISBN: 978-184831-204-3

Printed by Gutenberg Press, Malta

"It's Natural"

It is also a mistake, and a very frequent one, to use the word "natural" when we mean either <u>socially acceptable, morally desirable</u> or <u>aesthetically pleasing</u> – or, quite frequently, all three. The French radio station EUROPE 1 did this when it issued motorists with a sticker to put into the back of their car with an advertising slogan on it which read *EUROPE 1, c'est naturel*.

There is nothing **natural** about being a married Catholic with a lot of university degrees, and probably a lot of children as well. It is merely a statistical accident, a way of conforming which we owe to our birth and upbringing.

SOMEONE WHO, LIKE ME, WORKED AS A UNIVERSITY TEACHER, BUT WHO HAPPENED TO HAVE LIVED IN 19TH-CENTURY OXFORD, WOULD HAVE LOST HIS JOB IF HE HAD MARRIED.

AND WOULD NOT HAVE BEEN APPOINTED IN THE FIRST PLACE IF HE HAD BEEN A ROMAN CATHOLIC!

Mythologies

For Barthes, one of the greatest mistakes modern society makes is to think that its institutions and intellectual habits are good because they are in keeping with what is popularly called "the nature of things".

The second mistake is to see language as a natural phenomenon rather than a set of conventional signs. What Barthes wanted to do, as he said when discussing his aims in his best-known book, *Mythologies* (1957), was to "destroy the idea that signs are natural" (*battre en brèche la naturalité du signe*).

Saussure

FOR THERE IS, AS THE OBVIOUS IRONY OF BARTHES' QUESTION REMINDS US, NOTHING **NATURAL** ABOUT ONE'S RELIGION, ONE'S MARITAL STATUS OR ONE'S ACADEMIC ACHIEVEMENTS.

THEY ARE **SOCIAL CONSTRUCTS**, GIVEN TO US BY OUR RELATIONSHIP WITH OTHER HUMAN BEINGS, AND MEANINGFUL ONLY IN THE SOCIETY IN WHICH WE HAPPEN TO LIVE.

"I Have a Question to Ask …"

In 1975, when he was 62, Roland Barthes asked …

WHO DOES NOT FEEL HOW **NATURAL** IT IS IN FRANCE TO BE CATHOLIC, MARRIED, AND ACADEMICALLY WELL QUALIFIED?

Since he was himself a Protestant, a homosexual and had never taken a doctorate, his question was obviously an ironic and personal comment on himself.

More importantly, however, it underlined two of the main concerns running through the whole of his work: the need to distinguish between **nature** and **culture**; and the care we need to take in the *correct use of words*.

3

Thus, if we were to discover, after admiring a series of books extolling courage and marital fidelity, that the man who wrote them was a coward and a lecher, this would not have the slightest effect on their literary quality. We might regret his insincerity, but we should not be able to withhold our admiration for his skill as a writer.

But it is no more relevant to the literary quality of his books, or to their meaning, than the private life of a physicist is to the acceptability or otherwise of his views on the quantum theory or the structure of the atom.

Contre Sainte-Beuve

"The Death of the Author" underlines how important it is to distinguish between imaginative literature and autobiography. It is a distinction which is constantly blurred in the concept of literature developed in France in the 19th century by **Augustin de Sainte-Beuve** (1804–69), and against which Barthes' work can be seen as a permanent reaction.

FOR ME, THE PRINCIPAL AIM OF LITERARY CRITICISM IS TO FIND THE MAN **BEHIND** THE WORK ... AND THE MAIN CRITERION FOR JUDGING A WORK OF LITERATURE IS THE ACCURACY AND SINCERITY WITH WHICH THE WRITER TRANSLATES HIS **PERSONAL** EXPERIENCE INTO LITERARY FORM.

I STAND AT THE OPPOSITE EXTREME TO THIS IDEA, AND WOULD AGREE WITH THE ENGLISH POET **W.H. AUDEN** (1907–73) AND JEAN COCTEAU (1889–1963).

THE TRUEST POETRY IS THE MOST FEIGNING.

IL FAUT MENTIR POUR ÊTRE VRAI. (YOU MUST LIE TO TELL THE TRUTH.)

S/Z, 1970

S/Z, published in 1970, is one of Barthes' most difficult works. We can begin to understand it as a return once again to the **correct use of signs**, this time in the complex framework of Barthes' literary theory.

THIS WAS MY IN-DEPTH ANALYSIS OF THE WAY SIGNS WORK IN FICTION ...

I DEMONSTRATED THIS TO MY STUDENTS IN A CLOSE READING OF BALZAC'S STORY, "SARRASINE" ...

WHAT DOES PROFESSOR BARTHES CLAIM ABOUT FICTION WHICH DIFFERS FROM OTHER VIEWS?

Three Views on Fiction

We can offer three rival claims about the nature of prose fiction which Barthes criticizes and rejects in *S/Z*.

The first is from the author of the story himself, **Honoré de Balzac** (1799–1850). In his *Avant-Propos* (preface) to his great series of novels *La Comédie Humaine*, Balzac stated that he was not the real author of these books which depicted France in the late 18th and early 19th centuries.

PERSONALLY, I AM MERELY THE SECRETARY, TAKING DOWN WHAT FRENCH SOCIETY HAS DICTATED TO ME.

The English novelist **Hugh Walpole** (1884–1941) made a similar remark.

THE TEST OF A CHARACTER IN ANY NOVEL IS THAT IT SHOULD HAVE EXISTED BEFORE THE BOOK THAT REVEALS IT TO US BEGAN, AND SHOULD CONTINUE AFTER THE BOOK IS CLOSED.

And another English novelist, **Christopher Isherwood** (1904–86), expressed a complementary idea in his *Berlin Diary* (1930).

I AM A CAMERA WITH ITS SHUTTER OPEN, QUITE PASSIVE, RECORDING NOT THINKING.

The Mimetic Illusion

In each case, with Balzac, Walpole and Isherwood, the idea is that the novelist is copying or imitating a **pre-existent reality**, one which is totally independent of his own existence, and which there is only one natural way to express. This harks back to the ancient Greek concept of *mimesis* (imitation).

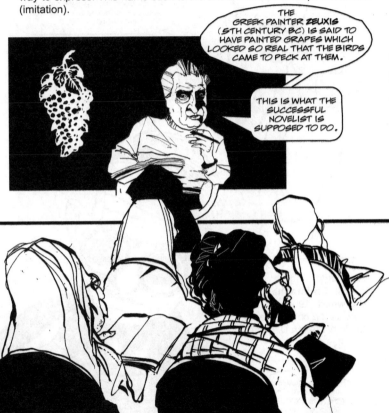

THE GREEK PAINTER **ZEUXIS** (5TH CENTURY BC) IS SAID TO HAVE PAINTED GRAPES WHICH LOOKED SO REAL THAT THE BIRDS CAME TO PECK AT THEM.

THIS IS WHAT THE SUCCESSFUL NOVELIST IS SUPPOSED TO DO.

But the **mimetic illusion**, in the theory of prose fiction which Barthes is attacking, works because the novelist had a real society, or a real person, to guide him in what he wrote; just as the painter had a real bunch of grapes to copy.

Barthes does not attack the mimetic illusion head-on by talking about all 80 or so volumes of Balzac's *La Comédie Humaine*, or even one of the best-known novels such as *Le Père Goriot* (1834) or *Illusions Perdues* (1837). He devotes all of the 85,000 words of *S/Z* to analysing the 10,000 words which make up a relatively minor short story, "Sarrasine", originally published in 1830, towards the beginning of Balzac's literary career.

The book is dedicated to the students who attended Barthes' seminars at the École des Hautes Études in 1968 and 1969, and is written, as Barthes rather nicely puts it, "*selon leur écoute*" (according to the way they listened to them).

But while this is, in a way, an ironic dig at the way in which a teacher as eminent as himself dominated his class, it also shows how little the events of 1968 had changed the nature of teaching in French higher education.

IN THE UNITED STATES OR THE UNITED KINGDOM, A GRADUATE SEMINAR IS ESSENTIALLY A PLACE WHERE STUDENTS INTERROGATE THE TEACHER AND CALL HIS IDEAS INTO QUESTION.

THIS DOES NOT HAPPEN IN FRANCE.

HERE, THE CONTINENTAL SYSTEM WHEREBY THE TEACHER TELLS HIS PUPILS WHAT'S WHAT, AND BROOKS NO REPLY, HAS REMAINED INTACT.

In another respect, however, *S/Z* shows Barthes as once again adopting to the study of literature a very different approach to the one which has traditionally dominated French education, both at the secondary and at the higher level. The traditional technique is known as the *explication de texte*, a method governed by two somewhat curious presuppositions.

A TEXT HAS ONE CENTRAL MEANING, WHICH IT IS THE DUTY OF THE CRITIC OR COMMENTATOR TO BRING OUT WITH ABSOLUTE CLARITY TO THE FULL LIGHT OF DAY.

AND THIS TASK IS NECESSARY BECAUSE SOMEHOW OR OTHER THE ORIGINAL AUTHOR HAS NOT QUITE MANAGED TO CARRY OUT THE TASK OF CLARIFICATION HIMSELF.

In *S/Z*, Barthes takes a completely opposite view.

THE MEANING OF A TEXT CAN BE NOTHING BUT THE PLURALITY OF ITS SYSTEMS, ITS INFINITE (CIRCULAR) TRANSCRIBABILITY.

The "death of the author", in Barthes' view of literature, has an immediate and liberating consequence: the **birth of the reader**. For Barthes, it is the reader who decides the meaning of a text. The reader is, naturally, guided by the signs which the author uses. But he or she is not held down by them. The reader can make, of the text, the meaning which the signs evoke in his or her mind and which can change from one day to the next, as well as from one reader to the next.

The Story of Sarrasine

The title *S/Z* is based on the two central characters in Balzac's short story "Sarrasine": the young French sculptor, Ernest-Jean **S**arrasine; and the person he falls in love with during a visit to Rome in 1758, a singer called La **Z**ambinella (the favourite of Cardinal Cicognara), whose beauty so inspires Sarrasine that he carves a statue of her in his workshop.

After a tumultuous party, Sarrasine abducts La Zambinella, only to discover that the singer is not a woman at all, but a *castrato*.

The Cardinal has Sarrasine assassinated, and his statue of La Zambinella goes on to inspire other works of art, in particular *Le Sommeil d'Endymion* (The Sleep of Endymion) by the French painter **Anne-Louis Girodet** (1767–1824).

The story of Sarrasine, La Zambinella and Cardinal Cicognara is told in flashback, at a party held in the house of the Comte and Comtesse de Lanty. The unnamed narrator is trying to seduce one of the guests, Madame de Rochefide.

It is, moreover, La Zambinella's immense fortune, acquired by a long and highly successful career in opera and on the stage, which has provided the basis for the even greater wealth of their hosts, the Lanty family.

Madame de Rochefide is so overwhelmed by the story that she refuses to keep her part of the bargain, and the narrator has told his story for nothing. He gets no reward.

I REFUSE TO SLEEP WITH YOU ...

This is the first way in which "Sarrasine", in Barthes' analysis of it in *S/Z*, is about nothing: a woman cannot be seduced by a story which revolves around the emptiness and lack of sex which characterizes **castration**.

The second is in Barthes' comment that Sarrasine dies "*d'un blanc dans le discours des autres*" (of a blank in the speech of other people). Because he is a foreigner, he does not know about the custom in 18th-century Italy which forbade women from appearing on stage.

HAD SOMEBODY TOLD ME ABOUT THIS, I WOULD HAVE KNOWN THAT LA ZAMBINELLA WAS NOT A WOMAN, BUT A CASTRATED MALE.

He would not, then, have tried to abduct "her", and Cardinal Cicognara would not have had him assassinated.

Sarrasine's life ends tragically because he does not know how other human beings have decided to manipulate the essentially arbitrary signs of feminine sexuality.

By analogy, this evokes the third concept in Barthes' analysis of "Sarrasine" which is linked with the theme of castration or emptiness: the nature of wealth in modern capitalist society.

The Lanty family is very rich – as, indeed, the ideal family in Balzac's world invariably is. But this money does not come from land, from work, or even from the solidity of real gold saved by their ancestors. It comes from the talent for singing which La Zambinella derived from the essential nothingness of "his" or "her" sexuality.

So, in the modern world of capitalist finance, of credit and of banking, wealth depends not on reality but on belief. If everybody were to decide to cash in their shares and draw their money from the bank, the system would collapse.

IT RESTS, AS THE SYMBOLISM OF CASTRATION MAKES CLEAR, ON AN **ESSENTIAL EMPTINESS**, ON AN ACT OF BELIEF IN A SYSTEM WHICH IS HIGHLY VULNERABLE, BEING BASED ON NOTHING MORE THAN A BELIEF.

From a literary point of view, however, which is Barthes' main preoccupation, it is the fourth concept associated with castration which is most important.

THE SUBJECT OF A WORK OF LITERATURE HAS NO MORE REALITY TO ITS MEANING OR VALUE THAN THE SEXUALITY OF A CASTRATO.

Zambinella

A work of literature may be very beautiful, and may contain interesting facts. One of these, which emerges from Barthes' analysis of "Sarrasine", and which would have delighted believers in the positivistic methods associated with **Gustave Lanson** (1857–1934), founder of the school of criticism to which Raymond Picard and his supporters tended to belong, is the detail it offers about the earning power of *castrato* singers in 18th-century Europe.

THE TALENT FORCED UPON LA ZAMBINELLA HAS, AFTER ALL, ENABLED "HER" TO LAY THE BASIS FOR THE IMMENSE FORTUNE OF THE LANTY FAMILY.

But a work of literature, as the whole analysis in *S/Z* tends to suggest, is also based on an **essential emptiness**. As in the case of the all-in wrestlers, there is nothing really there. Literature works, as Barthes puts it in *S/Z*, by exploiting the "plurality of its systems, its infinite (circular) transcribability".

A WORK OF LITERATURE CAN, IN OTHER WORDS, BE CONSTANTLY RE-INTERPRETED, OR RE-WRITTEN, IN THE MIND OF THE READER.

work

interpretation

This is particularly the case if the text is, as Barthes puts it, "*scriptible*" (writerly) – i.e. not so full of pre-existent meanings that it forbids all but one way of looking at it. Such a text, in Barthes' view, is merely "*lisible*" (readerly), requiring on the reader's part nothing but a passivity which prevents him from being conscious of the way it uses signs.

It is the **reader's freedom** which gives meaning to the text, not the author's intention, and not what earlier critics would have called its "content".

Sade, Fourier, Loyola

For the many admirers of Barthes, his book *Sade, Fourier, Loyola*, published in 1971, represents the compendium of the qualities in his writing and thinking which they most appreciate. The reason is that this book offers "case study" illustrations of the way in which structuralism can be made to work in a strictly literary context.

The **Marquis de Sade** (1740–1814), a relatively harmless sexual eccentric, wrote books describing imaginary universes in which unbelievable sexual orgies alternate with endless philosophical disquisitions. What interests Barthes is not the nature of the perversions enumerated by Sade or even their extreme improbability.

Charles Fourier (1772–1837), mathematician, geographer, failed merchant who hated industrialism, and bizarre social philosopher, wrote a number of utopian works describing imaginary societies in which men and women work together in total harmony.

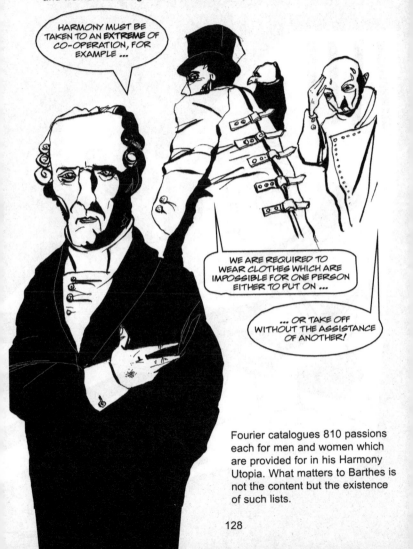

HARMONY MUST BE TAKEN TO AN **EXTREME** OF CO-OPERATION, FOR EXAMPLE ...

WE ARE REQUIRED TO WEAR CLOTHES WHICH ARE IMPOSSIBLE FOR ONE PERSON EITHER TO PUT ON ...

... OR TAKE OFF WITHOUT THE ASSISTANCE OF ANOTHER!

Fourier catalogues 810 passions each for men and women which are provided for in his Harmony Utopia. What matters to Barthes is not the content but the existence of such lists.

Again, for Barthes, what is interesting about Loyola is not his intense analysis of sins and various occasions of sin, but the fact that he **counts** them, and that the **self-contained world** which he describes can exist only in a confined and isolated place, like the imaginary "communities" that Sade and Fourier also describe.

Logothetes

Sade, Fourier, Loyola are, in Barthes' terminology, **logothetes**, meaning "founders of language". They are more than just authors of a system – Sadism, utopia, the Jesuit priesthood. Truly to found a new language requires, as Barthes says, **theatricalization**.

AND I DON'T MEAN SIMPLY DESIGNING A SET, BUT UNLIMITING THE LANGUAGE ...

Let's see what Barthes means by this "unlimited language" in each case.

Sade, Sadeanism

Sade's criminal eroticism is a system for which our society has no equivalent.

FOR ME, THERE IS NO EROTICISM UNLESS IT IS A REASONED CRIME ...

SADE PHILOSOPHIZES – HE SUBJECTS CRIME TO A SYSTEM OF ARTICULATED LANGUAGE.

"To reason" also means to combine the actions of vice according to precise rules, and to create from these series of actions a new language no longer spoken but acted – a new and elaborate **code** of love.

Sadean practice takes place in his various closed communities of the boudoir, remote castle, dungeon or even convent. It is formally regulated on a scale from the least detail of posture, as the "minimal unit", to the most complex combinations in orgiastic tableaux.

Sade's mania for numbers, calculations and codes was an obsession developed in the many years he spent in prison. One explanation was his need to keep a tally of what he called *prestiges*, orgasms achieved through masturbation or the use of instruments provided by his loyal wife Renée.

Because Sade frightens and disgusts us, he is often declared **monotonous**. Sade will appear monotonous and immoral to us, Barthes says, "only if we arbitrarily shift our reading from the Sadean discourse to the 'reality' it is supposed to represent".

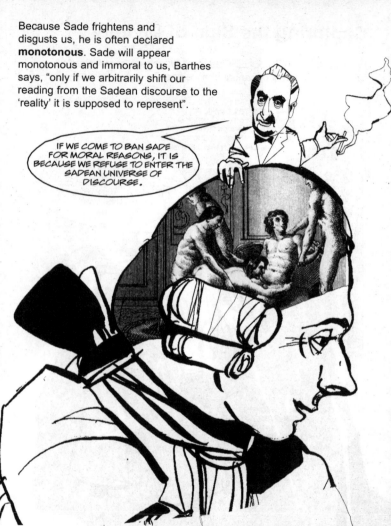

IF WE COME TO BAN SADE FOR MORAL REASONS, IT IS BECAUSE WE REFUSE TO ENTER THE SADEAN UNIVERSE OF DISCOURSE.

Sade always chooses the discourse over the referent: "He always sides with **semiosis** rather than **mimesis**." Barthes means that Sade is not a realistic author, one who "copies" or "refers" to the real, and we should not read him on that level of the "referent".

Capturing the Sign of Divinity

Ignatius of Loyola's book, the *Spiritual Exercises*, is described as "a universally extolled manual of asceticism".

IT IS A TEXT WHICH ADMINISTERS FOUR WEEKS OF CLOISTERED "RETREAT" – OF GRUELLING SPIRITUAL EXERCISES ON A JOURNEY THAT LEADS TO GOD.

"GOD" IN THIS SYSTEM IS THE DECODER OF THE EXERCITANT'S "MESSAGES" IN PRAYERS, MEDITATIONAL GESTURES AND PRACTICES.

Loyola's exercises are an art, Barthes says, "designed to determine divine interlocution". And as in Sade's strictly ordered theatre, Loyola's players inhabit a closed **written world**, a text, in which days, schedules, postures and diets are minutely regulated and dictated.

LOYOLA'S THEATRE, HOWEVER, IS ENTIRELY CREATED SO THAT THE EXERCITANT MAY REPRESENT **HIMSELF**.

HIS BODY IS WHAT IS TO OCCUPY IT.

In the isolated and darkened room in which he meditates, everything is prepared for the fantastic meeting of **desire** …

Placing himself before the Cross, the exercitant attempts to go beyond the signified of the image to its referent, the **material** Cross itself, perceived through the imagining senses.

In the terminology of semiotics, Loyola's discourse is **combinatory**, like a network of complicated branches that resembles a tree – as Barthes says, "a well-known figure among linguists". Here is a sketch of the First Week of exercises.

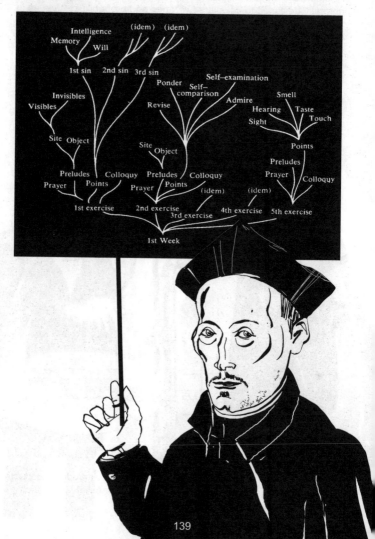

Inventing Harmony

Numbers in Fourier's utopian discourse are rarely statistical, that is, normally designed to calculate averages and probabilities. Just as in Sade and Loyola, numbers are **inventions**, quantities of "fantasmic detail" which have to do with Desire.

Let's look at a few of the "numbered details" of life as imagined in Fourier's utopia, Harmony.

Human Stature
In the Harmonian world, the height of "societary" man will reach 7 feet or 84 thumbs.

WHY 7 FEET? AND WHOSE "FOOT" IS THE MEASURE HERE?

32

1/2

THE FOOT OF THE KING OF PARIS IS A NATURAL MEASUREMENT. IT HAS THIS PROPERTY BECAUSE IT IS EQUAL TO THE 32ND PART OF THE WATER LEVEL IN SUCTION PUMPS.

This is the "metonymic" charm of Fourier: in the space of a few words, we have suction pumps mingled with the height of societary man.

Talents of Societary Man

Fourier invents by applying 810 – the number of the passions, if we recall – to exalt the possibilities of societary talents.

Mealtimes in Harmony

There are five meals in Harmony: the 5 a.m. matutinal, lunch at 8 a.m., dinner at 1, a snack at 6 and supper at 9, plus two collations at 10 and 4, reminiscent of the schedule in an old-fashioned sanatorium.

THIS MULTITUDE OF MEALS IS NECESSARY FOR THE RAVENOUS APPETITE THE NEW ORDER WILL CREATE.

ON THIS DIET OF HAPPINESS, HARMONIAN MAN WILL SLEEP ONLY FROM *11* IN THE EVENING TO *3.30* IN THE MORNING.

Sex

Everyone devotes a set part of the day to love, a principal business, which has its code, its tribunals, its court and its institutions.

A New Programme for Literature

Each of these three authors describes a world utterly improbable from any realistic or conventional view. Barthes seems to favour this form of writing and reject the content of traditional literature which Western culture has judged sane, interesting and valuable. He is suggesting a new, relatively unfamiliar and highly stimulating concept of literature.

WHY SHOULD A BOOK NOT BE SEEN AS THE EXPRESSION OF WHAT WE WOULD **LIKE TO BE**, RATHER THAN OF WHAT WE ARE OR HAVE BECOME?

BUT ISN'T SUCH A DESIRE UTOPIAN?

Barthes' imaginary, or even utopian, programme links up with the worlds that Sade, Fourier and Loyola have created through their books. It suggests a way of looking at literature which is initially surprising because it challenges the "canonical" idea of Western literature.

THE ONLY LITERATURE WORTH WRITING OR READING IS THE ONE THAT IS **ABOUT SOMETHING.** IN SHORT, IT IS **CONTENT** AND NOT **FORM** WHICH CREATES LITERARY VALUE.

COMING AT LITERATURE FROM A DIFFERENT ANGLE, I SUGGEST PRECISELY THE OPPOSITE!

Barthes, the Hedgehog

Up to now, in the first 16,000 or so words of *Introducing Barthes*, I have presented Barthes as a kind of hedgehog, interested to the point of obsession in one central idea: the view of literature as a sign system whose understanding depends not upon its content but on the **reactions** which the signs it exploits evoke in the mind of the reader.

I have done so for two reasons:

to **parry** the criticism frequently made of Barthes by English-speaking critics who reproach him with leaping from one subject to another and never presenting a coherent view of experience;

but also to **illustrate** what I think is a central idea running through his work and giving it a certain unity.

147

Outsider or Insider?

In spite of the vision which Barthes kept of himself until the end of his life of a man who was an outsider in French society, he did reach the top of the academic tree. In 1976, he was elected to the Collège de France; than which, as the English critic John Weightman pointed out, "there is no higher consecration here below".

Barthes was not, it is true, given a post at the Sorbonne. But he probably would not have accepted it, even if it had been offered to a man who had never done a doctorate, and had even written books without a bibliography.

But the Collège de France, created by the king François I in 1529 in order to provide a humanistic alternative to the outdated, theology-dominated teaching of the Sorbonne, had always had greater prestige among the leaders of French thought.

THE HONOUR WHICH I FELT HAD BEEN BESTOWED ON ME BY MY ELECTION WAS HEIGHTENED BY MY ADMIRATION FOR THOSE WHO HAD PRECEDED ME.

One great predecessor had been the historian **Jules Michelet** (1798–1874) on whom Barthes had himself published a book in 1954. He described Michelet in his 1977 inaugural lecture as the man in whom, at the very beginning of his intellectual life, he had discovered what he called …

… THE SOVEREIGN PLACE OF HISTORY IN THE STUDY OF MAN, AND THE POWER OF WRITING, ONCE SCHOLARSHIP ACCEPTS THAT COMMITMENT.

Also the philosopher **Maurice Merleau-Ponty** (1908–61).
And the historian of ideas **Michel Foucault** (1926–84).

Language and Literature

But his inaugural lecture also gave Barthes the opportunity to come back to the main preoccupation which runs through the whole of his work – the nature of language – and to express ideas about it which were, and remain, profoundly revolutionary – and perhaps even true. For what Barthes argued was that "language – the performance of a language system – is neither reactionary nor progressive; it is quite simply fascist; for fascism does not **prevent** speech, it **compels** speech."

Even if I were to decide that everything I have said is wrong, and re-write the book, I am still in the same situation. What I have written creates a system which cannot be **changed**. It can only be **questioned**.

IT IS A DEFINING CHARACTERISTIC OF LITERATURE THAT IT CONSTANTLY CALLS LANGUAGE INTO QUESTION. THIS IS ITS GREAT VIRTUE, AS WELL AS A REASON WHY THERE CAN NEVER BE A FINAL INTERPRETATION OF A WORK OF LITERATURE.

TEXTS ARE ALWAYS OPEN, ALWAYS SUBJECT TO BEING RE-WRITTEN IN THE MIND OF THE READER. LITERATURE IS THE PROOF AND THE ASSERTION OF HUMAN FREEDOM.

Barthes Visits Japan

In his *Structuralist Poetics* (1982), one of Barthes' most influential English-speaking admirers, Jonathan Culler, quotes a remark from **Friedrich Nietzsche** (1844–1900): "I fear that we are not getting rid of God, because we still believe in grammar." Barthes adopts exactly this attitude towards language in *L'Empire des Signes* (1970), his study of Japan, which he visited in the 1960s.

Even the sprawling, unmapped Japanese towns found favour in his eyes. Tokyo, for instance, did not seem organized around a solid circle of guaranteeing truth, but around an **emptiness** designated only by arbitrary signs.

THE EMPEROR OF JAPAN IS ANOTHER EMPTY SIGN ...

"The city I am talking about [Tokyo] offers this precious paradox: it does possess a centre, but this centre is empty. The entire city turns around a site both forbidden and indifferent, a residence concealed beneath foliage, protected by moats, inhabited by an emperor who is never seen, which is to say, literally, by no one knows who." Barthes refers here to the Emperor of Japan, **Hirohito** (1901–89), the former Sun God who was forced by the Allies to renounce his divine status after World War Two.

Japanese Poetry, Food and Sex

He liked the literary conventions of the Japanese *haïku* in which form is everything and content nothing.

On a withered branch
a crow has settled –
autumn nightfall.
Matsuo Basho (1644–94)

For, as he was to write in one of the later essays in the posthumously published collection *L'Obvie et L'Obtus* (1982), one of the advantages of the *haïku* was that it enabled language to cast off "the empirical yoke which reduces it to being merely a system of communication".

Already, in one of the essays in *Mythologies*, Barthes had expressed a dislike for the way French cooking, especially of the type advertised in women's magazines, tends to smother food in thick, smooth sauces, and his revulsion against this made him particularly appreciative of Japanese food. For Barthes had a strongly **hedonistic** streak to his personality. In 1972 he wrote an enthusiastic preface to a new edition of the *Physiologie du Goût* (1825) by French gastronome **Anthelme Brillat-Savarin** (1755–1826). Barthes also became increasingly open, in his later years, about his homosexuality.

Writing as Intransitive

But above all, he rejoiced in the presence of a sign system which was totally different from the one which prevailed in Europe. Nobody, he argued, looking at Japanese writing, could see it as embodying what he called "a metaphysics of presence".

NOBODY COULD ENTERTAIN THE TYPICALLY WESTERN IDEA THAT LANGUAGE IS GIVEN BY GOD AS A DIVINELY SANCTIONED MEANS OF COMMUNICATING EXPERIENCE.

IN JAPAN, I'M PHOTOGRAPHED TO *LOOK* JAPANESE!

When one of the critics writing about *L'Empire des Signes* said that it revealed Barthes' deepest ambition, that of "being able to write in Japanese without understanding the language", he was making a joke which had a certain truth in it. Barthes had always had the ambition not only, as he himself put it, of "destroying the idea that signs are natural", but of using signs for their own sake. Writing, he always insisted, is **an intransitive verb**.

A Childhood Snapshot

One of the features which distinguishes human beings from the other animals, Barthes maintained, was the fact of their having had a childhood, and in the personal note which he allowed to come into the later part of his work, he provided more and more details of how this was true in his case.

Barthes had a childhood dominated by genteel poverty. His widowed mother, Henriette, had to go out to work to provide money for herself and her son. Barthes gives a movingly honest account of how sad he was at the separation this implied.

157

On Photography

Henriette Barthes, whose death in 1980 cast Barthes into a state of depression which helped to bring about his own death, is also the person whose memory provides the starting point for Barthes' meditation on photography in what was the last book he published in his lifetime, *La Chambre Claire* (1980).

The photograph which he comes across of his mother as a young woman has the effect, as he puts it, of a "*punctum*", an image which pierces him to the heart, and does so for reasons which he had explored as long ago as 1961 in an essay entitled "The Photographic Message".

For what the unposed picture brought home to him, in addition to the reminder of the physical presence of the person in his life whom he had most loved, was the extreme rarity of an art form which merely showed **what was there**.

SOMETHING WHICH CONTENTS ITSELF WITH **DENOTING**, WITHOUT INTRODUCING ANY OF THE CONNOTATIONS WHICH PLACE MOST REPRESENTATIONS OF THE WORLD, WHETHER VERBAL OR VISUAL, IN AN IDEOLOGICAL CONTEXT.

Longing and Love

What emerges from Barthes' writings on photography is what one might call a kind of longing for an art form that is entirely pure in that it simply shows what is there. What he wants to escape from is the stifling presence of the supernumerary messages with which we overload and spoil our representation of the world.

In another intensely personal book, *A Lover's Discourse* (1977), Barthes shows – perhaps without entirely meaning to do so – just how deeply this experience of longing for his mother had affected his personal life.

TO LOVE IS ALWAYS THE DESIRE TO BE LOVED IN RETURN, TO HAVE THE PERSON WITH WHOM YOU FALL IN LOVE MAKE YOU FEEL, BY LOVING YOU, THAT YOU HAVE VALUE IN HIS EYES.

The verb "to ravish", as it is used to describe what the Romans did when they carried off the Sabine women in order to make them their brides, had also in Barthes' view a different meaning, and one which is emotionally more profound. For when I am "ravished" at the sight of another person, it means that I lose control of myself at the sight of the person I love.

Against the Dominant Ideologies

As in the case of money, Barthes maintains, the ideologies which seek to dominate our lives also try to do so by devaluing both sex itself and the love and pleasure which it can bring with it.

The great disadvantage of the three ideologies which dominated the 20th century is that each one of them pronounces a curse on money.

MARXISM SEES IT AS THE ORIGIN OF OPPRESSION AND CLASS PRIVILEGE, THE MEANS WHEREBY MEN ARE ALIENATED FROM THEIR OWN CREATION.

CHRISTIANITY TEACHES THAT IT IS THE ROOT OF ALL EVIL, AND PREACHES THE VIRTUE OF POVERTY.

WHILE FREUDIANISM ASSIMILATES IT TO FAECES ...

Each of them, Barthes argues, is wrong. Money not only gives freedom. It also offers a pathway to pleasure.

The Importance of Money

In the quest for pleasure, money is essential, and it is a subject on which Barthes writes with an acute sense of its importance. For instance, this is one of the advantages of prostitution …

In *Roland Barthes par Roland Barthes*, he spoke of "the goddess Homosexuality", and put forward a telling argument in favour of what are sometimes known as "perversions".

But it is in literature that Barthes insisted the greatest pleasure could be found – though not of the type traditionally attributed to it in Western society.

A Tradition of Explanation

It is Barthes' argument, and an important one, that Western literature went wrong when it based its approach to story-telling on the presentation of the Oedipus legend as dramatized by **Sophocles** (c. 496–406 BC) in Greek antiquity.

And just as literature in the Western tradition is essentially **explicative**, so Western society has an essentially **instrumental** view of language: as a tool to translate experience into rationally comprehensible terms. But this, maintains Barthes, is only one way of looking either at language or at literature. Like all our ways of thinking, this instrumentalist view of language is **culturally related**. It is a relative, not an absolute concept. And since Barthes' whole work is aimed at calling it into question, he cannot be criticized in terms of the very tradition which he is setting out to reject.

Sensual Production

The only way to approach Barthes is in the hedonistic view of language and literature which he sets out in *Le Plaisir du Texte* (1973). What matters, in the view of the mature hedonistic Barthes, is the meaning which it is possible to **produce sensually**. The best way of seeing what he means is to consider the implications of what he called, in an essay on the French singer Gérard Souzay, "*le grain de la voix*" (the texture of his voice).

THE GREAT MISTAKE MADE BY SINGERS SUCH AS DIETRICH FISCHER-DIESKAU IS TO SING IN SUCH A WAY AS TO BRING OUT THE **MEANING** OF THE WORDS AT THE EXPENSE OF THE **TEXTURE** OF THE MUSIC.

He illustrates this idea by writing, in *Le Plaisir du Texte*, a passage on the cinema, one which shows the mature Barthes at his best; and, oddly enough in the light of his insistence that language is *physical pleasure* and not *communication*, at his most persuasive.

Il suffit en effet que le cinéma prenne de très près le son de la parole (c'est en somme la définition généralisée du "grain" de l'écriture) et fasse entendre dans leur matérialité, dans leur sensualité, le souffle, la rocaille, la pulpe des lèvres, tout une présence du museau humain (que la voix, que l'écriture soient fraîches, souples, lubrifiées, finement granuleuses et vibrantes comme le museau d'un animal), pour qu'il réussisse à déporter le signifié très loin et à jeter, pour ainsi dire, le corps anonyme de l'acteur dans mon oreille: ça granule, ça grésille, ça caresse, ça rape, ça coule: ça jouit.

In fact, it is enough for the cinema to capture the sound of speech close up (that is, in fact, the generalized definition of the "grain" of writing) and make us hear in their materiality, their sensuality, the breath, the gutturals, the fleshiness of the lips, a whole presence of the human muzzle (let the voice, the writing, be fresh, supple, lubricated, delicately granular and vibrant as an animal's muzzle), for it to succeed in carrying the signified far, far away from us, and in casting, so to speak, the anonymous body of the actor into my ear: it granulates, it crackles, it caresses, it grates, it cuts, it comes: that is bliss.

The Death of Barthes

Barthes died on 26 March 1980 after having been knocked over by a laundry van in the rue des Écoles, just opposite the Sorbonne.

He had just had lunch with the philosopher Michel Foucault and the leader of the Socialist opposition François Mitterrand, who was to be elected President in the following May.

The accident had in fact occurred on 25 February. There were a number of press reports to the effect that Barthes had more or less let himself die because of the state of acute depression into which he had been plunged by the death of his aged mother, Henriette.

ROLAND BARTHES

People who didn't like Barthes made a point of getting an easy laugh by saying how odd it was that a specialist in signs should have failed to pay attention to the traffic around him. But reports of the accident suggested that the driver of the laundry van was drunk, which would not be an unusual condition after lunchtime in Paris.

Further Reading

The works by Roland Barthes currently available in English include the following, listed in chronological order of publication in French. Unless otherwise stated, the place of publication in France is Paris, and the publishing house is Éditions du Seuil.

Writing Degree Zero (*Le Degré Zéro de l'écriture*, 1953), translated by Annette Lavers and Colin Smith (Jonathan Cape, London, and Hill & Wang, New York, 1967). Republished 1984. The American edition has a long preface by Susan Sontag.

Michelet (*Michelet par lui-même*, 1954), translated by Richard Howard (University of California Press, 1988).

Mythologies (*Mythologies*, 1957), translated by Annette Lavers (Jonathan Cape, London, and Hill & Wang, New York, 1967). Republished 1990.

Critical Essays (*Essais critiques*, 1964), translated by Richard Howard (Northwestern University Press, Chicago, 1972).

On Racine (*Sur Racine*, 1965), translated by Richard Howard (Hill & Wang, New York, 1965, and Basil Blackwell, Oxford, 1992).

Elements of Semiology (*Éléments de Sémiologie*, 1965), translated by Annette Lavers and Colin Smith (Jonathan Cape, London, 1967, and Hill & Wang, New York, 1975).

Criticism and Truth (*Critique et Vérité*, 1966), translated by Catherine Keunemann (Athlone Press, London, and University of Minnesota Press, 1987).

Fashion System (*Système de la mode*, 1967), translated by Matthew Ward and Richard Howard (Hill & Wang, New York, 1983).

S/Z (*S/Z*, 1970), translated by Richard Miller (Jonathan Cape, London, and Hill & Wang, New York, 1975).

Empire of Signs (*L'Empire des Signes*, Skira, Geneva, 1970), translated by Matthew Ward (Jonathan Cape, London, and Hill & Wang, New York, 1983).

Sade, Fourier, Loyola (*Sade, Fourier, Loyola*, 1971) translated by Richard Miller (Hill & Wang, New York, 1976).

Pleasures of the Text (*Le Plaisir du Texte*, 1973), translated by Richard Miller (Hill & Wang, New York, 1975, and Jonathan Cape, London, 1976).

Roland Barthes (*Roland Barthes par Roland Barthes*, 1975), translated by Richard Howard (Hill & Wang, New York, 1977).

A Lover's Discourse: Fragments (*Fragments d'un discours amoureux*, 1977), translated by Richard Howard (Jonathan Cape, London, and Hill & Wang, New York, 1978).

Camera Lucida. Reflections on Photography (*La Chambre Claire. Note sur la photographie*, 1980), translated by Richard Howard (Jonathan Cape, London, and Hill & Wang, New York, 1981).

The Rustle of Language (*Le Bruissement de la langue*, 1984), translated by Richard Howard (Jonathan Cape, London, and Hill & Wang, New York, 1988).

The Responsibility of Forms. New Critical Essays on Music, Art and Representation (*L'Obvie et L'Obtus. Essais Critiques III*, 1982), translated by Richard Howard (Jonathan Cape, London, and Hill & Wang, New York, 1984).

The Grain of the Voice: Interviews, 1962–1980 (*Le Grain de la voix: entretiens 1962–1980*), translated by Linda Coverdale (Hill & Wang, New York, 1984).

Author's Warning to Students of Barthes

I have not mentioned another important result of the Barthes–Picard quarrel (page 80 ff.). This was to establish the view that Barthes could not be meaningfully discussed in the kind of "language of clarity" favoured by Picard and other traditional critics. Therefore, it is bad enough that I have referred in these pages to such empirical critics as L.C. Knights on *Macbeth*, or the poet T.S. Eliot and even the Romantic writer S.T. Coleridge, to illustrate the fact that some ideas championed by Barthes had been anticipated in the traditions of English literature.

I could have, but did not, mention other critical parallels. For instance, Barthes' crucial distinction between what an author *thinks* he is doing and the different meanings which his work can be *read* as having, is an argument for which there is a critical precedent. In an essay, "The Intentional Fallacy" (in *The Verbal Ikon*, 1954), the American critics W.K. Wimsatt and Monroe C. Beardsley argued that there was no way in which an author's intention could be taken as valid evidence of the *meaning* of the books he wrote.

I could also have suggested that Barthes is in the moralistic Protestant tradition of the Cambridge critic **F.R. Leavis** (1895–1976) or the essayist **George Orwell** (1903–50). Indeed, the comparison with Orwell is especially notable in that the accessibility of Barthes' writing on "pop subjects" in *Mythologies* (1957) is very like Orwell's critical essays (*Inside the Whale*, 1940, and *Shooting an Elephant*, 1950). What interested Orwell, in such essays as "Boys' Weeklies" or "The Decline of the English Murder", was how the value systems of contemporary society were reflected in popular culture. He found a brilliant disciple in **Richard Hoggart** (b. 1920), whose *Uses of Literacy* (1960) is a more systematic application of Orwell's methods to the magazines and popular newspapers of the post-war period, and which is also the English equivalent of *Mythologies*.

To write about Barthes in the style exemplified by Orwell or Bertrand Russell is, for his admirers, a total betrayal of his work. It is as though one were trying to explain Einstein in terms of Newtonian physics, or Darwin in the language of the Old Testament.

You have therefore been warned.

If you are going to be assessed by one of his admirers, whether in an examination or a prepared essay, **do not** write about Barthes in the way I do.

Choose, instead, to write:

as Stephen Heath does in **Reading Barthes** (Macmillan, London, 1977);

as Annette Lavers does in **Roland Barthes: Structuralism and After** (Harvard University Press, Cambridge, MA, 1982);

as Steve Ungar does in **Roland Barthes: The Professor of Desire** (University of Nebraska Press, Lincoln, NE and London, 1983);

or as Mary Bittner Wiseman does in **The Ecstasies of Roland Barthes** (Routledge, London and New York, 1989).

Do not do as I have done and try to reduce him to the simplistic, immediately comprehensible notions of middle-class English empiricism.

Do not, above all, try to translate his style of thinking and writing into the ordinary language so favoured by the society which defeated the student uprising of 1968.

Concentrate, instead, on the works that I do not discuss in any detail:

Michelet par lui-même (1954), translated by Richard Howard as *Michelet* (University of California Press, 1988);

Essais Critiques (1964), translated by Richard Howard as *Critical Essays* (Northwestern University Press, Chicago, 1972);

Nouveaux Essais Critiques (1972), translated by Richard Howard as *New Critical Essays* (Hill & Wang, New York, 1980);

L'Empire des Signes (1970), an essay on Japan, translated by Richard Howard as *Empire of Signs* (Jonathan Cape, London, and Hill & Wang, New York, 1982);

La Chambre Claire. Note sur la photographie (1980), translated by Richard Howard as *Camera Lucida. Reflections on Photography* (Jonathan Cape, London, and Hill & Wang, New York, 1982);

And, above all, the **Introduction à l'analyse structurale des récits** (1966), translated by Stephen Heath in *Image-Music-Text* (1977) and republished in Susan Sontag's comprehensive and invaluable *A Barthes Reader* (Jonathan Cape, London, and Hill & Wang, New York, 1982), which contains a translation of a wide variety of texts by Barthes, including his 1978 Inaugural Lecture at the Collège de France, and his 1961 essay, "The Photographic Message";

Roland Barthes, by Jonathan Culler (Fontana Modern Masters, London and New York, 1983);

Roland Barthes: The Figures of Writing, by Andrew Brown (Clarendon Press, Oxford, 1992).

Readers with a knowledge of French who are interested in a less enthusiastic approach to Barthes' work will find amusement and instruction in **Le Roland Barthes sans peine** by Michel-Antoine Burnier and Patrick Rambaud (Balland, Paris, 1983), and in the work of the Racinian scholar, René Pommier, who has devoted much of his career and a considerable amount of energy to denouncing what he sees as the errors of Barthes, Lucien Goldmann, Charles Mauron and other representatives of what was known in the 1960s as *"la nouvelle critique"*.

What these books have in common, whether written by Barthes himself or by his admirers, is that they are **not** reducible to summary in ordinary language.

They are, in contrast, what Barthes maintains literature should be: **autonomous creations** whose relation to ordinary life is, at the most, tangential; an idea admirably illustrated by the text of *Sade, Fourier, Loyola*. These books do not, unlike *Introducing Barthes*, have to be read like a comic, surreptitiously beneath the desk, as a crib to see what the lecturer is really saying.

Acknowledgements

Our thanks to Paul Cobley, author of *Introducing Semiotics*, for his contribution to "Reading the Elements", pp. 50–3.

The artist would like to thank Duncan Heath, Olivie for the photographic material he provided me with, and the people at Icon, and also wants to dedicate this book to all the seekers, especially Silvina.

Biographies

Until his retirement in 1993, **Philip Thody** was Professor of French Literature at the University of Leeds. He published books on Anouilh, Barthes, Camus, Genet, Huxley, Proust and Sartre. He is also the author of *Introducing Sartre*. He died in 1999.

Piero is an illustrator, artist and animator. His work has twice been included in the Royal College of Art in London. He is also the illustrator of *Introducing Shakespeare*, *Introducing Anthropology*, *Introducing Psychiatry* and *Introducing Nietzsche*.

Index

The Death of the Author

But as a literary theoretician, which is a role that he did fulfil, he is best known for an article first published in 1968 and called "The Death of the Author". In it, he argued that the very term *auteur*, with everything that it implies by way of a writer with a distinct personality which he expresses through his work, should be rejected and replaced by that of *scripteur*, simply **somebody who writes** – a being as impersonal as the letter-writer in cultures with a low level of literacy, a person endowed with the ability to handle a pen and prepared to do so for anybody but himself.

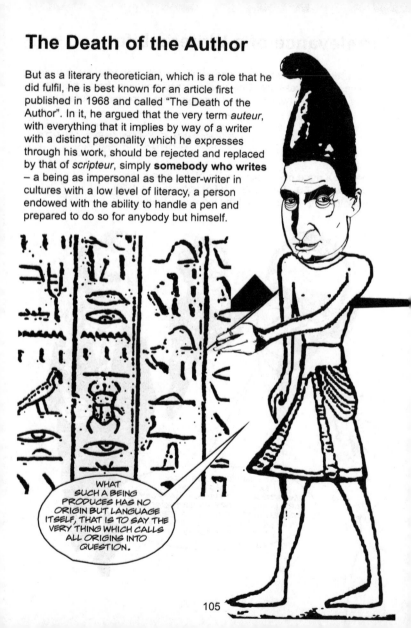

WHAT SUCH A BEING PRODUCES HAS NO ORIGIN BUT LANGUAGE ITSELF, THAT IS TO SAY THE VERY THING WHICH CALLS ALL ORIGINS INTO QUESTION.

Irrelevance of a Writer's Life

The "scriptor", in this respect, has within him "neither passions, humours, feelings nor impressions. Only this immense dictionary from which he takes an *écriture* (writing, verbal activity) which can never cease."

There is a more plainly put version of this idea in an essay which **T.S. Eliot** (1888–1965) published in 1920 under the title "Tradition and the Individual Talent".

LIFE DOES NOTHING BUT IMITATE BOOKS, AND BOOKS THEMSELVES ARE MERELY OBJECTS WOVEN OUT OF SIGNS.

IMPRESSIONS AND EXPERIENCES WHICH ARE IMPORTANT FOR THE MAN MAY PLAY NO PART IN HIS POETRY, WHILE THOSE WHICH BECOME IMPORTANT IN HIS POETRY MAY PLAY QUITE A NEGLIGIBLE PART IN THE MAN, THE PERSONALITY.

It is no more natural to listen to one radio station rather than another, just as it is no more natural to eat potatoes rather than spaghetti, to speak German rather than Hindi, or to prefer the theatre to the cinema.

It may well make life easier for us, if we live in a society like that of middle-class France, if we get married in church and work hard to pass examinations. But there is nothing natural about it.

All-In Wrestling

Most of the essays in *Mythologies* (1957) first appeared in newspaper form, many of them in the wartime Resistance publication *Combat*, whose first editor had been **Albert Camus** (1913–60). Although the essay "*Le monde où l'on catche*" (The world of all-in wrestling) was too long for a newspaper article, it does fit in with this aspect of Barthes' work by talking about a **popular**, non-intellectual activity.

IT IS PROBABLE THAT IN THE FRANCE OF THE 1950s, MORE PEOPLE ATTENDED ALL-IN WRESTLING MATCHES THAN WERE IN THE HABIT OF READING NOVELS OR GOING TO THE THEATRE.

WRESTLING ARENA

WRESTLING

CIVIC AUDITORIUM

TUES. JAN. 2

DeMARCO vs GOMEZ

TERRIBLE TED vs BEAUREGARDE
BASTINE vs GRAHAM

Barthes' essay is the best introduction to what he also thought went on in the mind of the reader of fiction or the play-goer.

Barthes points out, at the very beginning, that there is a fundamental difference between all-in wrestling and a genuine sport such as boxing or tennis.

IN BOXING, THE CONTESTANTS ARE REALLY HITTING ONE ANOTHER, AND BOTH ARE TRYING TO WIN.

ALTHOUGH THERE MAY BE SOME CASES WHERE A BOXER HAS DECIDED TO THROW THE FIGHT, THIS IS RELATIVELY RARE, AND IS NOT CENTRAL TO THE SPORT.

IN COMMERCIALLY ORGANIZED ALL-IN WRESTLING, IN CONTRAST, THE SITUATION IS TOTALLY DIFFERENT. IT IS NOT A GENUINE FIGHT, AND IT IS EASY TO SEE WHY.

Whereas professional boxers fight, at the outside, once every three months, all-in wrestlers give several performances a week. They <u>make no attempt to hide this fact</u>, and it is quite easy to follow them round as they go from town to town to give their <u>performance</u> …

Performance

And the word "performance" is the only way to describe what they do.

FOR IF THEY WERE **REALLY** DOING WHAT THEY ARE **PRETENDING** TO DO, THEY WOULD DO SUCH DAMAGE TO ONE ANOTHER THAT THEY COULD NOT POSSIBLY DO IT NIGHT AFTER NIGHT IN DIFFERENT TOWNS.

Moreover, Barthes argues, and this point is central to his argument, **the audience itself knows it is all pretence**.

Nobody is fooled; just as nobody was but the naive Victorian lady who leapt to her feet and shouted:

YOU GREAT, BIG, BLACK, FAT FOOL, CAN'T YOU SEE?

… when Othello was being driven into torments of jealousy by Iago.

This is why Barthes argues that the attitude of the spectator at an all-in wrestling match is so much like that of the reader of a novel or the spectator at a play. We all know, if we think about it for a moment, that there never was a David Copperfield or an Emma Bovary, and that it is all made up.

We know that the man playing Othello is not really a Moorish general in 16th-century Venice. He may not, now that it is normal to have a black actor playing the part, be covered in boot polish in the way that Laurence Olivier used to be. But he is **not** Othello, and he is not really murdering Desdemona; just as Giant Haystacks is not really trying to kill the Man in the Mask in an access of blind fury which leads him, apparently, to throw him onto the canvas from a great height and jump on him with all his massive weight.

Introduction to Structural Linguistics

In literature, to use the technical terms of the structural linguistics conceived by the Swiss linguistician **Ferdinand de Saussure** (1857–1913), there is no *signifié* (= signified) to which the signs refer back, no **guaranteeing centre of ultimate truth** which makes the signs work in the way they do.

IN THE PAST, THE VALUE OF THE POUND STERLING WAS GUARANTEED BY THE GOLD IN THE BANK OF ENGLAND, THAT OF THE DOLLAR IN THE VAULTS OF FORT KNOX.

NOW, ALL IT DEPENDS ON ULTIMATELY IS THE BELIEF WHICH PEOPLE HAVE IN THE STRUCTURE OF THE BRITISH OR AMERICAN ECONOMY.

In this respect, Barthes' essay on all-in wrestling is an application to popular culture of the theories of Saussure. For Saussure, the crucial distinction to be made when discussing language is between **the sign** and **the thing signified** – or as he put it in French, between *le signe et le signifié*.

THE LATTER, THE THING WE ARE TALKING ABOUT, REMAINS CONSTANT FROM ONE SOCIETY TO ANOTHER.

BUT THE LINGUISTIC SIGNS WE USE TO REFER TO THINGS DIFFER FROM ONE LANGUAGE TO ANOTHER.

How Do Words Mean?

A cow is the same, whether in England or France. But *vache* is not the same word as *cow*, and it is not some inner relationship between the words *une vache* and the animal in the field that makes them mean a cow, any more than it (the cud-chewing animal in the field) stands as a kind of guarantee that the letters c-o-w will always designate that beast and no other.

Words work in the way they do because of the place they have in the **structure** of the language, because they are different from one another and fit into a particular pattern.

Similarly, the gestures of the all-in wrestlers mean something, but not because of what the wrestlers themselves think or feel, which is probably something like...

The gestures derive their meaning from the conventions by which human beings have learned to express their own emotions and to understand those of other people.

Nature or Structure?

The wrestlers' gestures seem to be **natural**, in the same way as it seems to us natural to speak in English.

BUT ALL FORMS OF COMMUNICATION ARE ARTIFICIAL, SINCE ALL OF THEM WORK BECAUSE OF A STRUCTURE.

THE STRUCTURE CAN WORK ONLY BECAUSE WE LIVE IN SOCIETY AND NOT IN A STATE OF NATURE.

Not only, according to Saussure, is there nothing at all natural about *signs*, but they are also essentially **arbitrary**. Barthes' essay on all-in wrestling is a convincing statement of this view.

AT FIRST SIGHT, WE MIGHT SAY, ON WATCHING AN ALL-IN WRESTLING MATCH, IT IS ALL NATURAL, IN THE SENSE THAT WHAT WE CALL BRUTE VIOLENCE IS NATURAL.

IN FACT, WE COME TO REALIZE THAT IT IS ALL CAREFULLY, NOT TO SAY IMPECCABLY CODED ... JUST AS A SET OF SEMAPHORE SIGNALS IS CODED OR THE ANTICS OF A TICKTACK MAN AT A RACE COURSE ARE PART OF AN ELABORATE CODE.

Conventions of Performance

At times, the moves made by the wrestlers are even like a strange ballet, a carefully choreographed performance in which all the conventional signs for anger, frustration, vengeance and ultimate triumph are presented in a way which the wrestlers know that the audience will both understand and appreciate.

THERE ARE EVEN **SPECIFIC CONVENTIONS,** SUCH AS THE ONE WHEREBY A WRESTLER HELD ON THE CANVAS BY AN APPARENTLY EXCRUCIATINGLY PAINFUL ARM-LOCK INDICATES THAT HE IS NOT GOING TO GIVE UP.

I BEAT THE CANVAS WITH THE FLAT OF MY HAND!

If the conventions allowed it, and this was what the spectators were used to, he could indicate the same determination by pulling his left ear or shouting "God save Ireland!"

Barthes' importance as a writer about language lies in his ability to express Saussure's theory about the arbitrary nature of signs in the unexpected manner which he does in "*Le monde où l'on catche*".

He does so not in **abstract terms** but by talking about popular **everyday experiences**. And he does so like a skilful general who attacks the enemy at what seems to be his strongest point, which is in fact full of the weaknesses which show how vulnerable he really is.

Meaning and Differences

Anyone who had not read Barthes' essay, and was asked to give an example of the manifestation of brute force and anger in their crudest, most natural form, might well say, "Oh yes. I know. An all-in wrestling match."

After reading Barthes, that view is not so sure. The ambition to *battre en brèche la naturalité du signe* (destroy the idea that signs are natural) is achieved by analysing them when they appear to be at their most natural, but are, in fact, still what they always have been: parts of an elaborate, arbitrary and highly sophisticated **code**.

Saussure's basic contention was that what **creates meaning** inside a particular sign system is the differences between the terms used.

The two most frequent examples chosen to illustrate his ideas are traffic lights and the two English words "pin" and "pen".

The system, as such, would work just as well if STOP were indicated by a series of blue dots on a white background, and GO by a series of yellow lines against a black background. This difference would be enough, and indeed more than enough, to make the system work.

Again at first sight, an all-in wrestling match seems to contradict this idea that meaning is created by differences. It all looks so **natural**, even down to the physical appearance of the two performers.

Seeing is Believing?

So, when the good guy wins, as he is often allowed to do, the audience can feel that honour and fair play have been rewarded. But when, as is also sometimes allowed to happen, the bad guy wins, the audience can indulge in the even more agreeable emotion of **moral indignation**.

YET WHEN YOU THINK ABOUT IT, IT IS ONLY A SET OF CONVENTIONS ABOUT A PERSON'S PHYSICAL APPEARANCE WHICH MAKE US CREDIT HIM WITH A CERTAIN NUMBER OF MORAL CHARACTERISTICS.

A fine, upstanding-looking athlete can be just as vicious as a fat, slouching, apparently lazy yobbo. It is all in the **conventions**; and in the **differences** which leap so immediately to the eye.

When we think critically about the experience of watching an all-in wrestling match, we realize that we have been taken in. We have been made to think that certain ways of looking and of behaving are natural. In fact, they are **cultural constructs**.

Knowing It Is Different

It does not need much reflection about the nature of language to realize that Saussure is right, and to invent our own explanation as to why the word "pun" does not mean the same as the word "pan".

It is not that the first word refers back to a "punniness" in jokes depending upon the same word having two different meanings, and the second to a "panniness" in frying pans and saucepans. It is that the vowel "u" is different from the vowel "a", and is immediately **seen as different** by all speakers of English.

When we come to look for parallels to Barthes' idea on literature, it is quite easy to show that other people have thought about the problems in a very similar way, and reached similar – if less dramatically presented – conclusions.

It is essential to Barthes' analysis of all-in wrestling, and to the whole Saussurian theory of the **arbitrary nature of signs**, that the audience should not be taken in.

THERE IS A DIFFERENCE BETWEEN WATCHING A REAL FIGHT AND WATCHING A FIGHT ON STAGE IN THE THEATRE.

THE ENGLISH POET AND CRITIC **SAMUEL TAYLOR COLERIDGE** (1772-1834) WROTE ABOUT THIS AS EARLY AS 1817 IN HIS *BIOGRAPHIA LITERARIA*.

I CALL IT THE **WILLING SUSPENSION OF DISBELIEF** THAT CONSTITUTES **POETIC FAITH**.

When we go to the theatre, Coleridge pointed out, we know perfectly well with one part of our mind that the actors, as Hamlet put it, "do but murder in jest", and that nothing is real. But we pretend to ourselves that we do not know. We "suspend our disbelief". The paradox, as Hamlet also observed when talking of the behaviour of the Player-King, is that we can be moved to tears by something which we know to be **totally imaginary**.

WHAT'S HECUBA TO HIM OR HE TO HECUBA THAT HE SHOULD WEEP FOR HER?

Hamlet's question could apply just as well to the cinema-goer who weeps at the last scene of the film *East of Eden*.

James Dean, who plays the son who at last wins back his father's love, died over 40 years ago. But we are still moved, just as we can quite easily find ourselves shouting in impotent fury as the Man from the Mountains pins the Lone Ranger to the canvas in a remorseless and tormenting arm-lock which we know, with the other part of our mind, is not hurting him at all.

Art and Reality

Barthes is a writer obsessed by one of the great paradoxes of the human condition.

> WE CAN, THROUGH ART, BE INTENSELY MOVED BY SOMETHING THAT DOES NOT EXIST, NEVER HAS EXISTED, AND NEVER COULD EXIST.

The central idea in Barthes' essay on all-in wrestling is also intellectually important. What he wants us to do is maintain a clear distinction in our own mind between the events of real life and those presented to us in mass entertainment or imaginative literature.

Barthes is not the first writer to have made this distinction. It was expressed in its best-known form, as far as imaginative literature is concerned, in an essay published in 1923 by the Shakespearean critic **L.C. Knights**, entitled "How many children had Lady Macbeth?"

For as readers of *Macbeth* cannot avoid noticing, there is an inconsistency in the text between what Lady Macbeth says in Act I …

I HAVE GIVEN SUCK, AND KNOW HOW TENDER 'TIS TO LOVE THE BABE THAT MILKS ME.

… and Macduff's despairing comment on Macbeth himself, in Act IV …

HE HATH NO CHILDREN.

Mystery in the Macbeth Household

Macduff would be able to wreak appropriate revenge for the murder (on Macbeth's orders) of his own wife and child by killing Macbeth's offspring. If Lady Macbeth were speaking the truth in Act I, then there ought to be children around to enable him to do this. But since he can't, critics have argued, then there is some mystery in the home life of the Macbeths which has to be explained.

What L.C. Knights pointed out in his essay was that all speculation of this kind is a waste of time, an activity based on what a follower of **Ludwig Wittgenstein** (1889–1951) or **Gilbert Ryle** (1900–76) would call a *category mistake*.

THAT OF CONFUSING THE LANGUAGE WHICH WE USE TO TALK ABOUT EVENTS IN REAL LIFE WITH THE POETIC USE OF LANGUAGE CHARACTERISTIC OF IMAGINATIVE LITERATURE.

Ludwig Wittgenstein

A POEM WORKS NOT BY REFERRING TO WHAT ACTUALLY HAPPENED IN THE EXTERNAL WORLD, BUT BY CALLING INTO PLAY, DIRECTING AND INTEGRATING CERTAIN INTERESTS.

It takes the capacity of human beings to imagine what is not the case, and to accept as temporarily true something which never happened, in order to make a theatre audience or the reading public of a novel react and feel in a particular way.

Elements of Semiology

Barthes is formally indebted to Saussure (and other pioneering linguisticians) for his short but highly technical *Elements of Semiology* (1965). Barthes recognizes Saussure's central place in the development of modern linguistics, especially in his insistence on the idea of **structure**. Before the lectures which Saussure gave in Geneva, posthumously published as a *Course in General Linguistics* in 1916, the study of language as a general social phenomenon hardly existed.

LANGUAGE STUDIES HAD PREVIOUSLY EMPHASIZED EITHER GRAMMATICAL CORRECTNESS OR THE WAY IN WHICH A LANGUAGE SUCH AS FRENCH EVOLVED FROM THE VULGAR LATIN SPOKEN BY ROMAN COLONISTS TO THE LANGUAGE AS IT EXISTS TODAY.

Linguists, before Saussure, concentrated on how individual speakers pronounced the language – what Saussure called "*la parole*" (the word) – and very little on how the language worked here and now, the structure which made it (in Saussure's terminology) "*une langue*", that is, an organized structure of signs whose meaning depended on their differences from one another. Barthes, following Saussure and most other modern linguists, maintains that what is interesting about language is how the structure works.

The synchronic approach is seen as more interesting because almost all other communication systems are inevitably mediated through language.

Iconic, Motivated and Arbitrary Signs

The peculiarity of language, as Saussure emphasizes, is that its signs are essentially *arbitrary*. It is this which enables signs to be combined in so many ways to convey so many different meanings. However, in *Elements of Semiology*, Barthes introduced the more accurate and useful term of "motivated", implying that there is an explanation for the way certain visual signs work.

> THIS EXPLANATION CAN BE FOUND IN THE RELATION OF VISUAL SIGNS TO THE SOCIETY IN WHICH THE USERS AND THEIR AUDIENCE BOTH LIVE.

Barthes suggests that there are basically three types of signs – the **iconic**, the **motivated** and the **arbitrary**. They are not rigidly different from one another, but exist on a kind of sliding scale: those with only one function, the iconic, at one end, through to those almost infinite in their possible meanings, the arbitrary, at the other.

Closely associated to these, because carefully defined by accepted conventions, are marks of identity such as national flags or uniforms, but these begin to merge into the motivated when they give rise to the wearing of civilian clothes that have a complex but nevertheless very clear set of associations in the particular society in which they have grown up.

THE TRADITIONAL BLACK BOWLER HAT AND TIGHTLY FURLED UMBRELLA OF THE BRITISH CIVIL SERVANT IS AN EXAMPLE OF THE MOTIVATED.

It is possible to imagine the signs being used differently – as indeed they are in the 1971 film *A Clockwork Orange*, where the young urban tearaway Alex and his friends wear black bowlers.

THEY CARRY SO HEAVY A SET OF CONNOTATIONS THAT IT IS MISLEADING TO THINK OF THEM AS PURELY ARBITRARY.

But what is most unusual is to find a sign which is so absolutely natural as to be totally unambiguous.

A World Immersed in Language

> HUMAN BEINGS LIVE SO COMPLETELY IN A LINGUISTIC WORLD THAT THERE ARE VERY FEW SIGNS WHICH CAN WORK PROPERLY WITHOUT AN EXPLANATION IN LANGUAGE OF WHAT THEY MEAN.

Those that do, like the examples which Saussure himself gives – road signs and the Morse code – are extremely limited, and can give only a highly restricted set of messages.

Rapid as the laughter of the person seeing the cartoon may be, the sketch becomes meaningful only when this viewer provides himself – as almost everybody does – with a kind of *sotto voce* verbalized commentary on it to himself.

As soon as there is society, writes Barthes in a key passage of *Elements of Semiology,* using the typographical sign of italicization to bring out the importance of what he is saying, *every usage is converted into a sign of itself.*

Taboos

Nothing in society is ever meaningless, an idea illustrated by the fact that the area of intellectual inquiry most influenced by the development of semiology is the study of **taboos**.

It is extremely unlikely, for example, that the abstention of Jews from pork or of Muslims from alcohol originated in a desire to avoid food poisoning or drunkenness.

Since wine played so central a role in Christian ritual, its use having been consecrated by forming the substance of the first miracle, the transformation of water into wine at the marriage feast at Cana in Galilee (John I: 1–11), a ban on its consumption was a very convenient way for Muslims to show how different they were from Christians.

Jewish kosher laws
dietary SIGNS
taboos on pork, shellfish, mixing meat and dairy ...
body SIGNS ...
male circumcision, uncut hair and beard ...

Application of Barthesian semiology to the study of taboos underlines the essential distinction between physical facts and social institutions or events. While the former are inert and neutral, it is a defining characteristic of the latter always to be saying and therefore meaning something. The importance which taboos have as signs cannot be separated from their need to be **mediated through language and expressed by it**.

Beyond Saussure: Post-Structuralism

Barthes goes on to differ from Saussure. Saussure got it wrong when he claimed that linguistics would eventually become only a part of semiology or the general science of signs.

ON THE CONTRARY, IT IS MORE FRUITFUL TO LOOK AT THINGS THE OTHER WAY ROUND AND SEE SEMIOLOGY AS PART OF LINGUISTICS.

THE WORD FOR "ALCOHOL" IN ANY LANGUAGE STILL SIGNIFIES "PROHIBITED" FOR ME AS A MUSLIM.

Barthes moves on from Saussure, and this has sometimes led to him being referred to as a "post-structuralist". This means going beyond Saussure's view that the relationship between the sign and the thing signified is arbitrary. It is better to describe this relationship as **motivated**, which avoids both the implication that the relationship is a natural one and the suggestion, inseparable from "arbitrary", that it is irrational.

Barthes and Derrida

Barthes suggests that placing linguistic (or even non-linguistic) signs in their social contexts will explain how and why they work. This aspect of his thinking links him with other post-structuralists, especially **Jacques Derrida** (1930–2004).

Barthes does not go so far as Derrida.

I DO NOT, FOR EXAMPLE, GO SO FAR AS TO MAINTAIN THAT SINCE LANGUAGE IS CONSTANTLY IN A STATE OF FLUX, THERE IS NO SUCH THING AS THE MEANING OF A TEXT.

The Author

But aspects of this notion are potentially there in his insistence on how the "death of the author" creates the "freedom of the reader" (see page 105 onwards). In this respect, he is prepared to recognize, as Derrida is, that there is no final authority for deciding the meaning of a text, just as there is no final meaning attached to a sign.

There can be no final meaning attached to signs because they are constantly changing according to context.

In the code of spoken French, the rolled "r" is a perfectly ordinary part of the phonetic behaviour whereby a Frenchman from south of the Loire communicates his meaning.

ON THE PARISIAN STAGE, HOWEVER, BEFORE AN AUDIENCE WHOSE MEMBERS NORMALLY USE THE UVULAR "R" WHEN SPEAKING TO ONE ANOTHER, THE ROLLED "R" IS A SIGN OF RUSTIC STUPIDITY.

There are other cases in English as well as in French society where a way of speaking, dressing, eating or drinking can take on quite different connotations according to context.

47

Nothing More Natural

On the English as well as the French radio it is noticeably frequent for the weather forecast to be read by somebody with a pronounced *provincial* accent rather than with the standard, metropolitan one. Irrational though the custom is, it has an obvious semiological function.

One of the principal errors which Barthes attacks in his *Elements of Semiology* is the tendency to see language as a neutral means of communication, almost the equivalent of a set of mathematical symbols. Such is the view which the English playwright **Tom Stoppard** (b. 1937) puts into the mouth of the character Henry in his play *The Real Thing* (1982):

"WORDS ARE INNOCENT, NEUTRAL, PRECISE, STANDING FOR THIS, DESCRIBING THAT, MEANING THE OTHER, SO THAT IF YOU LOOK AFTER THEM YOU CAN BUILD BRIDGES ACROSS INCOMPREHENSION AND CHAOS."

Tom Stoppard

THIS IS THE MOST UNBARTHESIAN IDEA POSSIBLE, SINCE IT IGNORES THE WHOLE ROLE OF **CONNOTATION** IN LANGUAGE.

The Real Thing

WHAT DISTINGUISHES WORKS OF LITERATURE IS THAT THEY HAVE NO "SIGNIFIED" NOTHING TO WHICH THEY ULTIMATELY REFER. THEY ARE, IN A PARTICULAR SENSE, **NOT ABOUT ANYTHING**.

Reading the Elements

Elements of Semiology is a misleading title because it is anything but "elementary". Some clues on how to read this text would therefore be useful. Barthes' central argument is that all cultural phenomena are organized into their own languages. Another key idea is one we have already noted. Rather than language being one part of a general semiology, as Saussure suggested, Barthes insists that semiology is a part of language. What does this mean? In practice, it means to posit a **system** (like Saussure's *langue*) in contrast to the **manifestations** of that system (examples of speech, Saussure's *parole*).

Evidence of this contrast, for Barthes, can be found in the work of other French thinkers, for example, in the structuralist anthropology of **Claude Lévi-Strauss** (b. 1908).

THE **SYSTEM** OF A STRUCTURE OF KINSHIP MANIFESTS ITSELF AS **SPEECH** IN THE EXCHANGE OF WOMEN.

System and Speech

This fundamental separation of "system" and "speech" applies to other cultural artefacts. One example is **cooking**.

System	**Speech**
a) rules of exclusion (taboos)	e.g. family traditions, national traditions of cookery
b) oppositions (savoury/sweet)	
c) rules of association (at the level of the dish or the menu)	
d) rituals of use	

We could also apply this juxtaposition of system and speech to cars, furnishings or clothes. Let us consider the example of fashionable garments.

System	Speech
a) as written about	virtually none
b) as photographed	the model (although *this* model is the only manifestation of the system)
c) as worn in legitimate combination	actual combinations of garments

53

Semiology of Fashion

In a later and even more technical work, *Système de la Mode* (1967), Barthes shows in practice how semiology is part of linguistics. This is where his views differ from Saussure's.

What he did was to write not about fashion itself – in the sense of the clothes which the models were advertising – but about the language in which the clothes were described. Instead of giving an account of the clothes advertised in *Le Jardin des Modes*, *Elle*, *L'Écho de la Mode* and *Vogue* during a six-month period in the late 1950s, Barthes concentrated exclusively on the language used by the editors and fashion writers.

Semiology – or semiotics as it was named by one of its earliest pioneers, the American philosopher **C.S. Peirce** (1839–1914) – is a less austere and inaccessible discipline than one might gather from an attempt to understand Saussure or Barthes.

Linguistic content is not the sole object of semiological analysis. All kinds of signs can be analysed semiologically, as Barthes' study of clothes demonstrates.

THE POINT I MAKE IS THAT NOBODY CAN DRESS INNOCENTLY.

Codes and Conventions

The revolutionary artist who thinks he is dressing quite naturally by spending the day in torn jeans and an old sweater is observing a set of conventions which is just as **carefully coded**, and just as meaningful, as that of the conservatively-minded civil servant with his dark suit, white shirt, and college or regimental tie.

Taboos on Clothes

Whatever we wear has a message for society as a whole.

We can, if we wish, ignore this warning. But we then have to suffer the consequences in the image which we create of ourselves in the minds of the people looking at us.

The punk who puts safety pins in the lobes of his ears may not be able to explain his behaviour in the intellectual framework developed by the semiologists. But he is, in general, quite prepared to pay a certain social price, inasmuch as he is not reluctant to accept the disapproval which his appearance attracts from the tax-paying public. **George Orwell** (1903–50) commented of the goose-step in *England, Your England* (1941):

ITS UGLINESS IS PART OF ITS ESSENCE, FOR WHAT IT IS SAYING IS "YES, I **AM** UGLY, AND YOU DAREN'T LAUGH AT ME", LIKE THE BULLY WHO MAKES FACES AT HIS VICTIM.

(Un)Conscious (Self-)Image

I AM MAKING MYSELF UGLY, AND THAT IS BECAUSE I HATE YOU. I AM ALSO MAKING MYSELF HIGHLY VULNERABLE. I KNOW THAT IT WILL CAUSE ME GREAT PAIN IF YOU GRAB HOLD OF THESE PINS AND PULL THEM. BUT YOU DAREN'T DO IT. YOUR SOCIETY HAS REJECTED ME, BUT YOU CAN EXPRESS THIS REJECTION ONLY IN YOUR TERMS. YOU HAVEN'T THE GUTS TO CONFIRM THIS REJECTION IN MY TERMS, WHICH ARE THOSE OF PHYSICAL VIOLENCE.

The semiology of everyday life, of which Barthes can be seen as the founding father, is above all else a school of intellectual honesty. It involves first and foremost the recognition that nobody should be unaware of the fact that the signs whereby they project their self-image onto the world are the expression of a conscious choice.

The Semiology of Everyday Life

Another example of the semiology of everyday life was provided by a Dominican priest known as **L'Abbé Pierre** (Henri Grouès, b. 1912). He suddenly became a well known media celebrity in Paris by the campaign which he launched, during the bitter winter of 1952, to save the down-and-outs who slept under the bridges in Paris from being frozen to death.

IT WAS A USEFUL AND CHARITABLE THING TO DO, AND BOTH L'ABBÉ PIERRE AND THE CHURCH DERIVED GREAT PRESTIGE FROM THE OPERATION.

But L'Abbé Pierre also had a superbly short haircut and a flowing, apostolic beard. Together they proclaimed with apparent naturalness his indifference to the conventions of the modern world and his zeal for the Christian ideal.

BUT THE BEARD AND HAIRSTYLE WERE IN THEIR WAY JUST AS CONVENTIONAL A SET OF SIGNS AS THE DARK SUIT AND DOG-COLLAR BY WHICH CLERGYMEN USED TO PROCLAIM THEIR CALLING.

The difference was that L'Abbé Pierre's beard and haircut were **dishonest**. They pretended to be *natural* when they were in fact highly *artificial*, as conventional a set of signs as the garb in which the all-in wrestlers give their performance.

61

Sartre's Concept of "Bad Faith"

Philosophically, and especially in the form which he gave to the analysis of the semiology of everyday life, Barthes' attitude towards signs has analogies with the concept of "bad faith" developed by his near-contemporary, **Jean-Paul Sartre** (1905–80).

Sartre argued that human beings are always free, and always know that they are free, but are always trying to pretend to themselves that their actions are pre-determined.

IF WE FREELY DECIDE TO DO SOMETHING, THEN WE AND WE ALONE ARE RESPONSIBLE FOR ANY RESULTS WHICH OUR ACTIONS MAY HAVE.

SO, TO AVOID THIS RESPONSIBILITY, WE CONSTANTLY PRETEND TO OURSELVES THAT OUR DECISION WAS NOT FREE, AND THAT IT IS CIRCUMSTANCES AND NOT OURSELVES THAT ARE TO BLAME.

I'M JUST OBEYING ORDERS.

Sartre calls this **bad faith**, and we can often catch ourselves out in it.

WE ARE ALWAYS CONSCIOUS OF THE EFFECT THAT THE WAY WE DRESS HAS ON OTHER PEOPLE.

BUT WE TRY TO PRETEND THAT IT IS **NATURAL** AND **SPONTANEOUS** TO WEAR THE CLOTHES WE DO. THEY EXPRESS THE CONSCIOUS, CULTURALLY-DETERMINED CHOICE WE MAKE AND THE WAY WE WANT OTHER PEOPLE TO SEE US.

Barthes' semiology of everyday life is inseparable from the Sartrian vision of human freedom, and of the responsibility which we have for the choices we make.

Just as there is, for Sartre, no such thing as a "human nature" which makes us into the people we are, so Barthes argues that this is also true for the way we look. Just as we choose the kind of person we wish to become, so we choose the way we communicate through the way we dress, as well as through the way we speak.

Understanding Barthes in Context

It is important to recognize that Barthes is very much of his time, again like Sartre and Albert Camus, and especially of that crucial period in France that went from the German Occupation of 1940–44 to the student rebellion of 1968.

Two features are particularly distinctive of that time and of Barthes himself: a sympathy for Marxism and a tendency always to present the working class in favourable terms, and the middle class – or the bourgeoisie, as Barthes invariably calls it – in unfavourable ones.

"BOURGEOIS" AND "PETIT BOURGEOIS", USED AS ADJECTIVES OF DISAPPROVAL, REVEAL A SET OF FRENCH ATTITUDES.

THE WORKING-CLASS AUDIENCE THAT GOES TO ALL-IN WRESTLING MATCHES IS AT LEAST HONEST WITH ITSELF. IT KNOWS IT'S ALL A GREAT CON, AND APPRECIATES IT AS SUCH.

The bourgeois theatre-goer, in contrast, who admires an actor or actress and wants to see what they are like "in real life", is far less honest and far less perceptive.

Barthes and Brecht

Barthes is profoundly French. His intellectual references are almost invariably French and his examples only very rarely taken from any literature other than that of France. One notable exception is Barthes' espousal of the German playwright **Bertolt Brecht** (1898–1956).

From 1953 to 1957, he led a veritable campaign in favour of Brecht, whom he was later to describe as …

SOMETHING OF A RARITY: A MARXIST WHO HAD THOUGHT ABOUT THE VALUE OF SIGNS.

In May 1954, the visit to Paris of Brecht's Berliner Ensemble offered Barthes an ideal opportunity to explain his admiration for a writer whose appeal also lay in his rejection of a theatre based on money. The Berliner Ensemble could put on plays that the working class could afford to go and see, because it was heavily subsidized by the government of the German Democratic Republic (a.k.a. East Germany, now deceased).

Unlike Camus and Sartre, Barthes never used his literary work to talk openly about politics. But he had, like the vast majority of 20th-century French authors, considerable sympathy for the views of **Karl Marx** (1818–83). Without ever being a Marxist, he shared with Marx's disciples and followers a strong dislike of the middle class, and a view of the literature of the past as reflecting the class conflicts of its time.

I DESIRE TO SEE WRITERS MAKING THEIR AUDIENCE MORE CONSCIOUS OF THE KIND OF SOCIETY IN WHICH THEY ARE LIVING.

Brecht's "Distancing Effect"

Views like this made Brecht's plays a perfect example of the kind of literature he admired, especially since the performances by the Berliner Ensemble, coupled with Brecht's own view of the theatre, corresponded so closely with Barthes' vision of **how signs work in literature**. The term used by Brecht to express his view of the theatre was the *Verfremdung*, or "distancing" effect, a style of acting which Barthes presents as having the great quality of preventing the audience from forgetting that it is all an illusion.

There is an obvious similarity between the essays which Barthes wrote on Brecht in the early 1950s for a review called *Théâtre Populaire* and the wrestling essay in *Mythologies*.

IN WRESTLING AND IN BRECHT'S THEATRE, THE AUDIENCE IS NEVER SO CAUGHT UP AND ABSORBED IN THE ACTION THAT IT LOSES ITS FREEDOM.

For the great defect of bourgeois art, in Barthes' view, is its tendency to convince the reader or spectator that it is all real, and thus to maintain the illusion that signs are natural.

WHEN ONE SEES AN ACTRESS PLAYING THE ROLE OF MOTHER COURAGE IN THE WAY THAT BRECHT INTENDED, THERE IS NEVER ANY DANGER OF THIS.

AT NO POINT DOES THE IDEAL BRECHTIAN ACTOR EXPECT THE AUDIENCE TO IDENTIFY OR SYMPATHIZE WITH HIM.

The Romantic concept of sincerity – of the actor moving the audience because he is moved himself – is at the furthest possible remove from the aesthetic which Barthes derives from Brecht's theory and practice in the theatre.

Against Clarity

Barthes was already a well known figure in French intellectual life by the time *Mythologies* appeared in book form in 1957. In 1953 he had published *Le Degré Zéro de l'Écriture* (*Writing Degree Zero*) in which he had marked himself out as a rebel in the French literary world by rejecting the idea that the most important quality in a work of literature written in prose was **clarity**.

Since the 17th century, and especially since the publication in 1674 of the *Art Poétique* by **Nicolas Boileau** (1636–1711), every pupil in every French secondary school has been made to learn Boileau's couplet …

*Ce que l'on conçoit bien, s'énonce clairement,
Et les mots pour le dire arrivent aisément.*

IF YOU THINK OUT JUST WHAT YOU WANT TO SAY, THE WORDS WILL COME WITHOUT THE LEAST DELAY.

NOT AT ALL! IN FACT, A LOAD OF BOURGEOIS RUBBISH!

Clarity is not an absolute, indispensable quality in prose. It is a **class attribute**, a way of writing which serves as a sign that you are a member of a particular class speaking to other members of the same class.

Clarity is, Barthes insists, no more a universal and universally desirable quality than the habit of reading a page of prose from left to right. Arabic-speaking cultures get on perfectly well by reading from right to left.

IT WAS ONLY WITH THE BEGINNING OF THE RISE TO POWER OF THE BOURGEOISIE IN 17TH-CENTURY FRANCE THAT THE KIND OF CLARITY ADMIRED BY THE FRENCH MIDDLE-CLASS ESTABLISHMENT TOOK ON THE IMPORTANCE WHICH BOILEAU AND OTHER THEORETICIANS PROCEEDED TO GIVE IT.

Later in his career, in 1978, Barthes went even further in claiming a positive privilege for what he called *illisibilité* (unreadability). It was, he said, a Trojan horse in the fortress of the human sciences.

By writing in a way which avoided the trap of conventional French clarity, writers could do more than destroy the idea that signs were natural ...

THEY COULD ALSO BREAK THE HOLD OF THE BOURGEOISIE ON THE WAYS OF THINKING ABOUT ECONOMICS, PHILOSOPHY, SEMIOTICS OR SOCIOLOGY WHICH ENABLED IT TO REMAIN IN POWER.

Not everyone agreed with this rejection of the idea which, since the publication in 1784 of *Discours sur l'universalité de la langue française* (Essay on the Universality of the French Language) by **Antoine Rivarol** (1753–1801), has also been accompanied by the belief that the French language has a clarity after which lesser tongues such as English, Latin or Greek aspire in vain.

Barthes' rejection of what he saw as the conventional idea of clarity nevertheless remained constant in his work, and links him with four other 20th-century thinkers who dominated French intellectual life in the 1960s.

ALL FOUR OF US, LIKE BARTHES, WERE ASSOCIATED WITH THE STRUCTURALIST MOVEMENT.

ALL FOUR, BY THE WAY WE WROTE, REJECTED THE CONVENTIONAL IDEA OF FRENCH CLARITY.

Anthropologist **Claude Lévi-Strauss** (b. 1908)

Psychoanalyst **Jacques Lacan** (1901–81)

ALL FOUR OF US INSISTED, AS BARTHES DID, ON THE OUTDATED NATURE OF MUCH FRENCH THINKING ABOUT LANGUAGE, LITERATURE AND SOCIAL CUSTOMS.

AND, LIKE BARTHES, I MADE NO SECRET OF MY HOMOSEXUALITY.

Philosopher **Jacques Derrida** (1930–2004)

Intellectual historian **Michel Foucault** (1926–84)

73

Against Realism

For the Barthes of *Le Degré Zéro de l'Écriture*, there is no such thing as a natural or realistic style of writing. The novelist who makes his characters say "fuck" or "shit", or who describes what they eat or wear, is not really "telling it how it is".

SINCE THE PEOPLE HE IS CLAIMING TO DESCRIBE NEVER EXISTED, HE COULDN'T BE. HE IS WRITING IN A PARTICULAR CODE: THAT OF THE **REALIST NOVEL**.

Realism, like all literary genres, is made up of a series of conventions: rude words, grinding poverty, brutal gestures, sexual depravity, intense human interest, unhappy marriages, a sordid background and an atmosphere of acute misery.

Realism is held together by the knowledge, shared from the start by reader and writer, that everybody is going to come to a sticky end, and quite probably a bloody one as well.

THESE CONVENTIONS ARE NO MORE REALISTIC THAN THE SHEPHERDS AND SHEPHERDESSES OF THE 17TH-CENTURY PASTORAL.

OR THE HANDSOME YOUNG DOCTORS, PRETTY NURSES, AND DISTRAUGHT-BUT-FINALLY-RESCUED PATIENTS OF TELEVISION SOAPS ABOUT HOSPITALS.

Is There a Natural Style?

In 1953, as the title *Le Degré Zéro de l'Écriture* suggests, Barthes did see one way of escaping from the artificiality which affects all types of writing, and which he explained in personal terms in *Roland Barthes par Roland Barthes* (1975).

One solution, he suggested in 1953, lay in the kind of writing practised by Albert Camus in his first novel, *L'Étranger* (*The Outsider*), in 1942: a totally neutral, deadpan style, like the one developed by **Ernest Hemingway** (1899–1961), or implied in George Orwell's famous remark: "Good prose is like a window pane."

By 1970, the year in which Barthes published *S/Z*, he had come to recognize this hope of a straight, natural and direct style as an illusion. As the Irish playwright **Oscar Wilde** (1854–1900) once remarked …

BEING NATURAL IS ONLY A POSE, AND THE MOST IRRITATING ONE I KNOW.

The only solution, as Barthes had already maintained in one of the essays that make up *Le Degré Zéro de l'Écriture*, is to adopt the motto of the Roman actor.

LARVATUS PRODEO (I ADVANCE, POINT TO MY MASK).

Since no human being can speak or write with the naturalness that characterizes an animal running or a fish swimming, the only honest thing to do is never pretend that what you wear, say or write is anything but part of a conventional code.

Origins of a Dramatic Contest

To appreciate Barthes, "the outsider", we must understand not only his non-Catholic background and homosexuality, but his peculiar relation to the Parisian academic establishment.

In France, teachers in the state system are civil servants, and the most prestigious jobs are reserved for those who have succeeded in the very difficult competitive examination called the *Agrégation*. In May 1934, Barthes had fallen ill with tuberculosis and in 1937 had been declared unfit for military service.

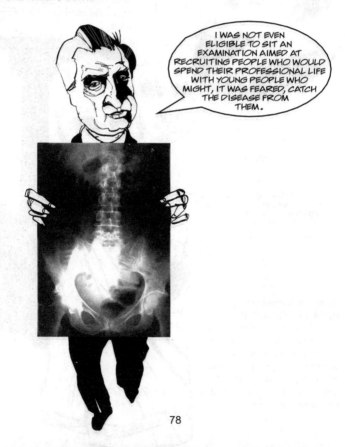

The Sorbonne and its Rival

University posts were reserved for those who had spent up to ten years writing a thesis known as the *Doctorat d'État*.

NEITHER *LE DEGRÉ ZERO DE L'ÉCRITURE* NOR *MYTHOLOGIES* WAS SEEN AS SERIOUS ENOUGH TO JUSTIFY EVEN A JUNIOR TEACHING POSITION AT THE SORBONNE.

After what Barthes euphemistically termed a period of "professional instability", in which his lack of more than a very basic university degree proved something of a disadvantage, he was appointed head of the Sixth Section at the École Pratique des Hautes Études, an institution founded in 1886 in order to serve as a rival and alternative to the Sorbonne.

The Racine Business

Now the stage was set for a dramatic contest which was triggered by Barthes' publication of a book, *On Racine* (1963), and the attack on it by **Raymond Picard** (b. 1917) in a pamphlet, *Nouvelle critique ou nouvelle imposture* (New Criticism or the Latest Intellectual Fraud).

Picard himself was very much an establishment figure: Professor of French Literature at the Sorbonne and author of a brilliant thesis entitled *La carrière littéraire de Racine* (The Literary Career of Racine). He was not, as some of Barthes' more enthusiastic supporters maintained, a man of the Right. During the German occupation of France between 1940 and 1944 he had played an active role in the Resistance movement.

THE ARGUMENT WITH RAYMOND PICARD WAS, AMONG OTHER THINGS, A DISPUTE BETWEEN **TWO ACADEMIC INSTITUTIONS** IN FRANCE.

AS WELL AS BETWEEN **TWO WAYS OF LOOKING** AT LITERATURE.

Picard had not personally sought the publicity set off by his criticism of Barthes. The essay in which he attacked Barthes had originally appeared in *La Revue des Sciences Humaines*, an academic publication with a circulation of some 5,000 subscribers. But it had been spotted by Jean-François Revel, one of the most intelligent and irreverent of French columnists.

I WAS KEENLY AWARE OF HOW MUCH THE FRENCH LOVE A GOOD LITERARY QUARREL!

It was, thus, by something of an accident that Picard's criticism placed Barthes in a position which he had neither sought nor foreseen: that of a victim of the French academic establishment whose persecution came to be seen, in the light of the student rebellion of 1968, as one of the reasons why this revolt had been so justified.

Understanding Racine

Picard represented the traditional view of **Jean Racine** (1639–99): the greatest of French dramatists, the epitome of French classicism. According to this point of view, Racine knew exactly what he was doing with every word he wrote. He rejoiced in the discipline of literary rules to the point where he exploited them for all they were worth.

Racine enjoyed a highly successful career as a writer of tragedies, which went from the triumphant first performance of *Andromaque* in 1666, through his brilliant analysis of the politics of imperial Rome in *Britannicus* in 1669, to culminate in his masterpiece, *Phèdre*, in 1677.

Racine's five-act tragedies were all written in rhyming couplets.

IN ORDER TO AVOID THE IMPRESSION OF PRODUCING A FORCED OR ARTIFICIAL RHYME, I FOLLOWED THE CUSTOM OF WRITING THE SECOND LINE FIRST.

He wrote all of his tragedies out in prose before putting them into the twelve-syllable Alexandrines which were the accepted poetic form, and took his subjects either from Greek antiquity, Roman history, or, in the case of his one excursion into the modern world, *Bajazet* (1672), the distant land of Turkey.

We know little of Racine's private life, apart from the fact that after a period of youthful dissipation, he married an extraordinarily dull woman who brought him a large dowry, bore him seven children, and never went to the theatre or read a line of his plays.

Although he somehow managed to incur the displeasure of Louis XIV, he had earlier amassed so many royal pensions that he died the equivalent of a millionaire.

The three essays which Barthes published on Racine in book form in 1963 presented a very different picture from the playwright whom French critics celebrate as the paragon of French dramatic art.

Totem and Taboo

Barthes followed the views set out by **Sigmund Freud** (1856–1939) in *Totem and Taboo* (1913).

THE CRUCIAL EVENT IN THE EARLY HISTORY OF HUMANITY WAS THE REVOLT OF THE SONS WHO GANGED TOGETHER TO EXPEL OR MURDER THEIR FATHER, THE TYRANT OF THE TRIBE.

WE WISH TO DESTROY HIS MONOPOLY OF THE SEXUAL FAVOURS OF THE WOMEN OF THE TRIBE.

BUT MY DOWNFALL DID NOT BRING HARMONY.

The sons quarrelled about who should then possess the women, and human history became the series of crimes and acts of violence which remain its dominant feature.

AND IT WAS THIS PATTERN, REMAINING IN OUR COLLECTIVE SUBCONSCIOUS, WHICH WAS REPEATED IN ALL OF RACINE'S TRAGEDIES.

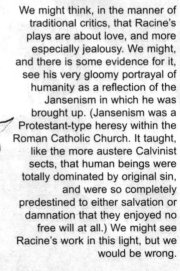

We might think, in the manner of traditional critics, that Racine's plays are about love, and more especially jealousy. We might, and there is some evidence for it, see his very gloomy portrayal of humanity as a reflection of the Jansenism in which he was brought up. (Jansenism was a Protestant-type heresy within the Roman Catholic Church. It taught, like the more austere Calvinist sects, that human beings were totally dominated by original sin, and were so completely predestined to either salvation or damnation that they enjoyed no free will at all.) We might see Racine's work in this light, but we would be wrong.

What, for Barthes, matters in Racine, and what the critic has to bring out, is the **unconscious structure** which dominated his mind. It was this structure which produced the work that interests us, and which it is our task to bring out to the full light of day.

WWHAT CHARACTERIZES THE WORLD OF RACINE IS THE CONSTANT REPETITION OF THE PATTERN WHEREBY "A" HAS ALL POWER OVER "B", BUT IS NOT LOVED IN RETURN.

It is a world dominated by the relationships of power and jealousy created by the original rebellion of the sons against the father. It is a world which Racine depicted **without realizing what he was doing**.

It would be misleading to pretend that *On Racine* is Barthes' best book. It is, as Picard argued, a highly simplified view of Racine, and is ridden with a rather pretentious jargon. It is not likely to increase anybody's enjoyment of the actual performance of any of Racine's plays, and Barthes gave something of a hostage to fortune when he confessed in the third of the essays that he did not actually like going to see *Andromaque* or *Phèdre* in the theatre.

The quarrel which it provoked with Picard, and with which virtually every critic in France joined in, is nevertheless important for three reasons.

It inspired him to write a reply to Picard, *Critique et Vérité* (*Criticism and Truth*) (1966), which explored the whole question of what literary criticism is, what it might be, and more particularly what it should be in a period of history which has witnessed so many changes in other fields of intellectual inquiry.

It consequently placed Barthes in the centre of an international debate about the nature of literature itself, and brought out the similarity between some of his views and those developed by critics writing in English. With the quarrel about Racine, Barthes became much more of an international figure.

It also made Barthes something of a martyr, and created the situation where it became very difficult for anyone writing about him in non-Barthesian terms to obtain a hearing from his supporters.

Without in any way having sought such a position, Barthes became an emblematic figure, the symbol of a revolt against the way in which bourgeois society preserved and discussed its cultural heritage, and how this society cast into the outer darkness anyone who dared to challenge its hegemony.

Goldmann's View of Racine

Barthes was not the only French writer to challenge the traditional view of Racine's plays. We can see the influence of two other critics on Barthes.

One of these was the Marxist critic **Lucien Goldmann** (1913–70), who published a long book entitled *Le Dieu Caché* (*The Hidden God*) in 1954. In it, he too argued that Racine did not really know what he was doing, and interpreted his tragedies as a transposition of the ups and downs of the Jansenist movement in its tumultuous and eventually disastrous relationship with the French crown. For in 1713, Louis XIV finally turned against it.

 Speech bubbles: "I ORDERED ITS FOLLOWERS TO ACCEPT THE CONDEMNATION ALREADY ISSUED BY ROME, AND CLOSED DOWN THE MONASTERY AT PORT-ROYAL DES CHAMPS ..." "... WHERE I HAD BEEN A SCHOOLBOY."

For Goldmann, the success of the Jansenist movement among the intellectual élite of 17th-century France had been due to the appeal which it made to a particular social class, and one to which its major ideological spokesman, the mathematician and philosopher **Blaise Pascal** (1623–62), as well as Racine himself, belonged by birth and upbringing.

This was the group of lawyers who purchased their offices from the King, and acquired at the same time the right to hand them on to their children.

FROM *1636* ONWARDS, I BEGAN TO HAND MORE AND MORE OF THE ADMINISTRATION OF THE COUNTRY TO MY PERMANENT CIVIL SERVANTS.

WE FOUND OUR POWER REDUCED AND THE VALUE OF THE INVESTMENT MADE BY THE PURCHASE OF LEGAL OFFICES CONSIDERABLY DIMINISHED.

AND SO WE TURNED TO JANSENISM ...

The Motive of Jansenism

Why turn to Jansenism? Because, in Goldmann's view, Jansenist theology emphasized the powerlessness of the individual soul in its relationship to God. The relationship to the King of the holder of a legal office in France was remarkably similar.

I TOO HAVE NO MEANS OF INFLUENCING THE DECISIONS WHICH AFFECT MY FATE IN THIS WORLD.

Structurally, the two situations were the same, and the relationships in Racine's plays mirrored them both.

For Goldmann, works of art existed in their own right. But they derived their **significance** as well as their **structure** from the way in which they enabled members of a social group to make sense of their experience.

The influence of *Le Dieu Caché* on Barthes is obvious. Not only does Barthes follow Goldmann's definition of tragedy as the realization by the individual that true values cannot be achieved in this world. He also accepts the same presupposition as Goldmann that the author is never fully conscious of what he is doing.

RACINE MAY, WITH HIS CONSCIOUS MIND, HAVE THOUGHT THAT HE WAS FOLLOWING IN THE FOOTSTEPS OF THE GREAT TRAGIC WRITERS OF CLASSICAL GREECE.

I BECAME THE FRENCH EQUIVALENT OF EURIPIDES (484-406 BC).

What he was really doing, in Goldmann's view, was expressing the world view of a class condemned by history to the same kind of political impotence that Euripides' heroes and heroines experience in their relationship to the gods.

Racine may, again with his conscious mind, have been trying to analyse why the sexual passions are so destructive, and to do so in verse of such perfection that it would ensure him a place among the immortals, as well as election to the Académie Française and the highly profitable favour of the King.

WHAT HE WAS REALLY DOING WAS MIRRORING THE PREHISTORY OF HUMANITY AND REPRODUCING THE PATTERNS WHICH, WITHOUT OUR REALIZING IT, STILL DOMINATE OUR OWN EMOTIONAL LIVES.

Mauron's Freudian View

The other critic who influenced Barthes was **Charles Mauron** (1905–70), whose study of Racine had been inspired by Freudianism. Unlike Barthes, and unlike Goldmann, Mauron considered that a writer's personal life had a direct influence on the books he wrote. Indeed, such was his whole thesis in *L'Inconscient dans l'Oeuvre et La Vie de Racine* (1957) – *The Unconscious in the Work and Life of Racine*.

WITHOUT KNOWING IT, THE MOST LUCID OF OUR WRITERS MODELLED HIS WORK ON AN UNCONSCIOUS OF WHICH, IN THE COURSE OF HIS CREATION, HE ATTAINED AN INTUITIVE KNOWLEDGE OF WHICH HE WAS NOT AWARE.

The Orphan Jansenist

For Mauron, as a convinced Freudian, the key to the understanding of anyone's personality lies in their early childhood. That of Racine was dominated by the fact that both his mother and his father died before he was three years old.

I WAS BROUGHT UP BY AN AUNT, AND EDUCATED AT THE JANSENIST SCHOOL AT PORT-ROYAL DES CHAMPS.

Love, Hate and Rebellion

There, in addition to his excellent knowledge of Greek, he acquired a deep emotional understanding of Jansenism, while at the same time coming to look upon the school, as orphans often do, as a substitute for the parents he had lost. But all children, as Mauron points out, have the same ambivalent attitude towards their parents. They love them, but they need to assert their independence by rebelling against them:

An Obsessive Pattern

It is, in Mauron's view, Racine's love–fear relationship with the Port-Royal of his childhood which explains the recurrence in his tragedies of the pattern by which a passionate, possessive woman falls in love with a man, finds that he cannot or will not love her in return, and either voluntarily or involuntarily brings about either his physical or his emotional or moral death.

IT HAPPENS IN ANDROMAQUE (1666), WHERE HERMIONE HAS HER ADORED PYRRHUS KILLED BY THE MAN WHOM SHE CANNOT LOVE, ORESTES.

RATHER DEAD THAN SEE HIM MARRY THE WIDOWED ANDROMAQUE.

It happens in *Britannicus* (1669), where Agrippine cannot let go of her son Nero and virtually forces him into crime.

It happens in *Bajazet* (1672), where Roxane, realizing that Bajazet will never love her, prefers to have him killed rather than see him marry his beloved Atalide.

And, most significantly, it happens in Racine's most famous play, *Phèdre* (1677), where Phèdre brings about the death of her stepson, Hippolyte, with whom she has fallen so passionately in love that she cannot bear the idea of his belonging to anyone else.

...es does not openly borrow either Mauron's Freudianism or ...mann's Marxism. But he has clearly been greatly influenced not ...by both ideologies, but by the idea which both critics share: that ...s do not, in the last analysis, understand their own work.

...leads him to argue, in *Critique et Vérité*, that any approach to the ...ture of the past, as of the present, **cannot** be based upon the idea ...Picard accepts without ever calling into question.

YOU HAVE TO TAKE AN AUTHOR ON HIS OWN TERMS, AND LOOK AT HIM IN THE LIGHT OF WHAT HE THOUGHT HE WAS DOING, THE AIMS AND AMBITIONS WHICH HE HAD CONSCIOUSLY IN MIND.

INSTEAD, YOU HAVE TO ADOPT A FAR MORE OPEN-MINDED APPROACH. ONE WHICH TAKES ACCOUNT OF WAYS OF THINKING BY WHICH WE NOW TRY TO UNDERSTAND OUR OWN EXPERIENCE: **MARXISM**, **FREUDIANISM**, AND **STRUCTURALISM**.

Gramsci's Theory of Hegemony

Barthes' quarrel with Picard was far more than a storm in an academic teacup. It was far too closely related to French intellectual life in general, and thus to French society itself, to be trivial. What it provided in the 1960s, and still provides now, is a specific example of the claim made about the nature of power in society by the Italian Marxist **Antonio Gramsci** (1891–1937), imprisoned under Mussolini's fascist regime in 1926, and who wrote and died in prison.

THE GROUP IN POWER IN SOCIETY ALWAYS INSISTS THAT INTELLECTUAL DISCUSSION SHALL TAKE PLACE IN THE KIND OF LANGUAGE WHICH IT USES, WHICH IT UNDERSTANDS, AND WHICH REPRESENTS ITS WAY OF SEEING, INTERPRETING AND DOMINATING THE WORLD.